explore

Introduction

Out of the sea, came the beginning.

These shores, these shimmering sands, these mosaics of rock were surrounded for millions of years by a silence broken only by the sea's ominous voice.

 The first man to add his puny noise as he scavenged along the beach for food lived days measured by the sun and moon and knew little but the drive of hunger and survival.

Man arrived in the Highlands and islands some 10,000 years ago. To him, the sweeping slopes and high buttresses of Glencoe would have been beyond reach.

The land could have had no quality but its harshness. Rocks of strange formation and water that crashed roaring into gulleys he must have regarded only as barriers. The barren tops he could rarely have trod and then only in dire emergency.

Forests gave him shelter, treating him no differently from the lynx, bear and wolf with which he competed for food.

Only after he had settled in communities did early man learn to save and, therefore, explore. Exploring is a luxury afforded after capital in energy, time and material is secured beyond that minimum needed to get through the day, the season, the year.

What little margin that was scraped together, then as now, was devoted to improving the home. Skara Brae in Orkney, with its primitive version of today's urban flats, testifies to that.

In the aftermath of fleeing, storm-driven, from their home the villagers of Skara Brae could not dream that it would take a similar tempest, thousands of years later, to expose their built-in, stone furniture to the sight of man once more.

In that time man had placed many shapes upon the landscape. Most of them bore the ancient traces of treaties negotiated with the environment. The steps at Whaligoe in Caithness, treading down the cliff face to the harbour, the derricks, the salt and net stores are perhaps an exception where man seemed to be the victor. But only for a while.

Man and his work are only tolerated. What he has taken for his own amounts to no more than a slim foothold between the ravages of the sea and the inhospitality of the brooding hills.

Yet, forced by nature, and at one time, by his stronger fellows, to live there, he can harvest both.

Sources in the past of lead, iron ore —and gold —the mountains now mean hydro power, winter sports, nature reserves, and mammoth water filled basins. The sea, once an obstacle and an accidental provider of food, now is alive with oilmen and fishermen armed with costly technology.

Generations have found nature a little kinder in some places, their energies producing a wealth that pleases the eye as well as the bank account.

Much of the area's agricultural produce is exported. So, too, are the salmon netted by the fishermen of Staffin in Skye. The protein captured in this environment is translated into human energy in distant, crowded cities.

The ruined shed which overlooks the coble's comings and goings is a reminder of other endeavours. In busier days it housed the machinery which helped load diatomite onto waiting vessels.

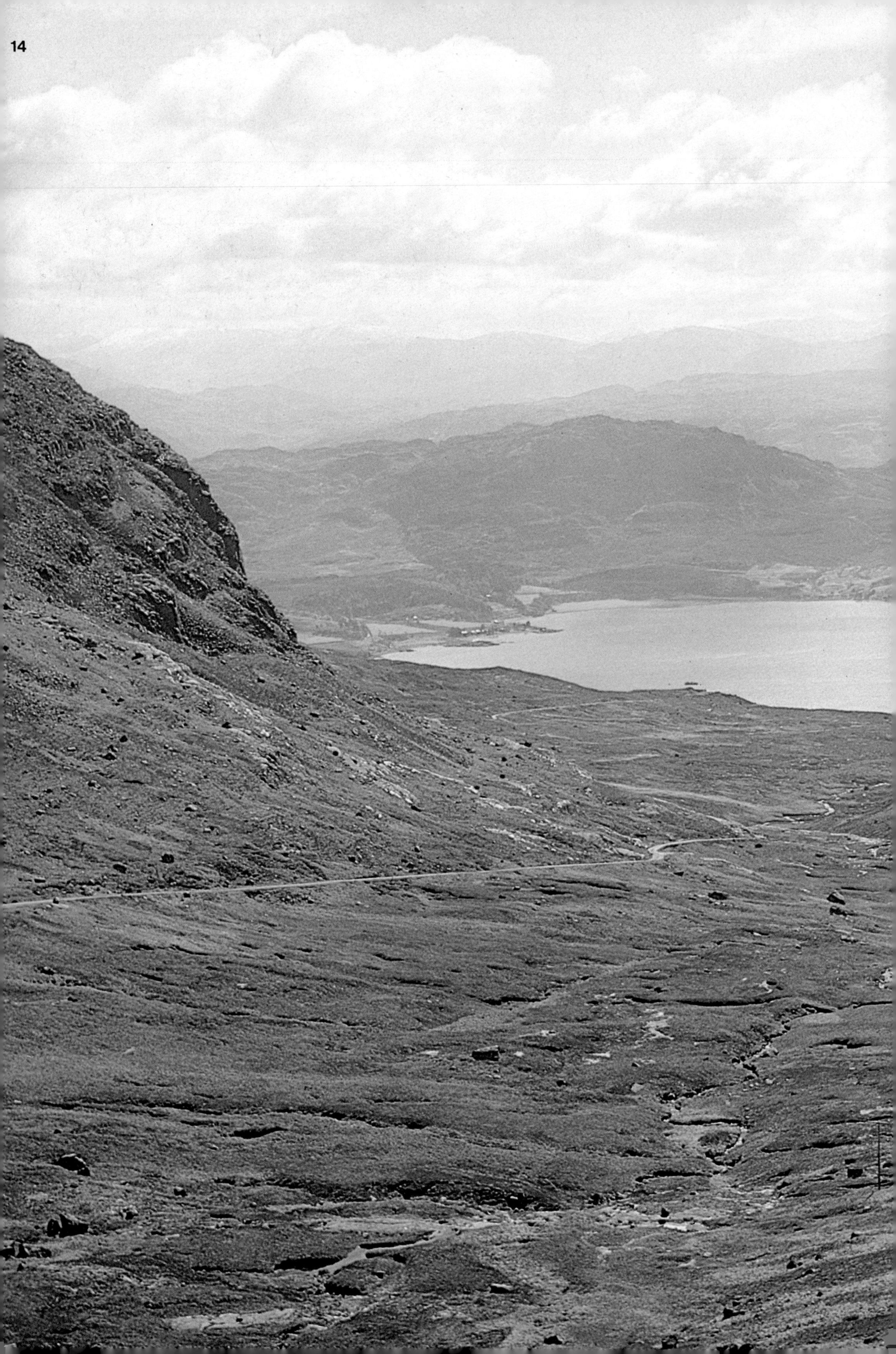

For nearly two centuries the wealth of the Highlands and islands had four legs and was driven to markets in the south through gaps in the mountains like the Pass of the Cattle in Wester Ross. The Scottish blood of the trader who blazed the Chisholm Trail to Abilene in Texas could well have coursed through an ancestor who drove cattle in their thousands from the Highlands to markets at Crieff, Falkirk and south of the border. Separated by time and the Atlantic, the patterns of their daily lives were much the same.

Now cars traverse the high road to Applecross, diesel-engined trains cross the Clava Viaduct, car ferries ply to the islands and back, and international flights touch down at Dalcross. They form a network which makes the high passes and low-lying islands accessible as they have never been before to all who wish to explore.

The Scottish novelist George Blake was not indulging in fictional licence when he saluted Arran as 'a great arrogant lion of an island'. It was an accurate description of this rampant Highland interloper in the Lowland waters of the Firth of Clyde. The thrusting peaks of Arran are authentically Highland, asserting a spectacular dominance over the Firth, and providing a dramatic flight marker for the transatlantic jets as they swoop in from the west to Prestwick airport.

The mountainous north of the island abounds in sheer rock faces, overhangs and ridges that would test the nerves and reflexes of the most experienced climber. Goatfell rises 2,866 feet, and Caisteal Abhail, Beinn Tarsuinn, Cir Mhor, Beinn Nuis, Beinn Bharrain, Am Binnearn, Cioch na h'Oighe, Beinn a Chliabhain and Suidhe Fhearghis all top the 2,000 feet mark. Truly, a rampant lion of an island.

Arran lies fourteen miles off the well groomed Ayrshire shore, its western coast shielded from the Atlantic by the protective arm of the long Kintyre peninsula. Across the Sound of Bute to the north are the Isle of Bute and the beckoning hills of Cowal. Given such a location, Arran has served as a stepping stone for successive waves of invaders, from the earliest mesolithic hunters to the neolithic people who buried their dead in chambered cairns; the Irish immigrants who established Dalriada, first Kingdom of the Scots; and the Norsemen. The Norse occupation of Arran can be traced in place-names, burial mounds, and runic inscriptions on the wall of a cave on Holy Isle.

In 1307 Robert the Bruce and his band of followers had a brief respite on Arran before taking up arms against the invading English. Twelve years after the Battle of Bannockburn—the one the Scots won—Bruce returned to the island, this time to engage in the kingly pursuit of hunting the red deer. The fourteenth century was also notable for Arran in the founding of Brodick Castle, and the emergence of the House of Hamilton as the island's most powerful family.

By a shrewd combination of perfidy and a cold eye for a good marriage—essential qualities in medieval times for nobles avid for advancement—Sir James, the first Lord Hamilton, acquired substantial holdings of land in Arran, His first wife was Euphemia Graham, daughter of the Earl of Strathearn, and widow of Archibald, fifth Earl of Douglas. Lord Hamilton joined the confederacy formed by his new kinsman the sixth Earl of Douglas against James II, then switched to the King's side, and was rewarded with lands forfeited by the Douglas family when the Earl was executed for treason. With his star firmly in the ascendant, the astute Lord Hamilton played his masterstroke. In 1474, he took as his second wife Princess Mary, eldest daughter of James II, sister of James III, and widow of Thomas Boyd, Earl of Arran.

Lord Hamilton's son by his second marriage—another James—was a chip off the old block. James received a grant of the Isle of Arran in 1503, becoming Earl of that Ilk. Despite falling into disfavour with the formidable Henry VIII, he saved his head and succeeded in furthering the family fortunes. Other scions of the House of Hamilton were not so fortunate. It is unlikely that they would have met with such violent ends if they had sat at home in Brodick Castle instead of pursuing their vaulting ambitions far from Arran.

The Earl of Arran's bastard son John seemed set for a glittering career when he became Archbishop of St Andrews. But in 1571 he was

Arran

executed, in his pontifical robes, on the common gibbet of Stirling. James, the third Earl of Arran, became unhinged by Queen Mary's rejection of his proposal of marriage, and was declared insane. The second Marquis of Hamilton died in Whitehall at the age of thirty-six, and was thought to have been poisoned by Buckingham. James, the first Duke of Hamilton, was executed for treason in 1649 in Palace Yard, Westminster. The second Duke was mortally wounded at the Battle of Worcester, and the fourth Duke—a noted duellist—was slain in a duel in Hyde Park. There was no consolation for him in the fact that the result was a draw, his adversary—Lord Mahon—also expiring.

Historic Brodick Castle is now owned by the National Trust for Scotland, Standing amid wooded grounds overlooking the sandy sweep of Brodick Bay—Arran's chief port of call—the castle houses the prized Hamilton collection of sporting prints and silver, as well as many art treasures. The sumptuously furnished dining room and drawing room illuminate the life-style of the departed Dukes of Hamilton. Brodick Castle gardens extend to sixty glorious acres; the exquisite formal garden being the culmination of devoted care from the year 1710.

There are no towns on Arran, and none of the seedy commercialism associated with some Clyde resorts. The scatter of villages around the coast are wholly in accord with their rural setting, as the climbers, hill-walkers, anglers, golfers—Arran has seven golf courses—and family parties who return again and again will gratefully attest.

From Lamlash—where the graceful crescent of Hamilton Terrace surveys the calm waters of the broad bay under the massive shield of Holy Isle—the coast road runs south by Whiting Bay and Kildonan to Lagg before circling north through Corriecravie, Blackwaterfront and Machrie to Lochranza.

The ruined square keep in Lochranza bay watches the comings and goings of the summer car ferry to Claonaig in Kintyre. There are few who take that ferry who will not be drawn back to the unspoilt glens, sandy bays and quiet creeks of Arran under the imperious peak of Goatfell.

18 Once Henry Bell's steamship, the *Comet*—belching such ominous black clouds of smoke that watchers on the Bute shore took to the hills in fear of their lives—had surmounted the hazards of her maiden voyage, the revolution in sea transport was safely under way. Within decades, Bell's inventive genius led to the launching of holiday travel into an untapped mass market. The lure of cheap transport galvanised Glasgow's industrial workers, penned in their grim sandstone tenements. They streamed 'doon the watter' in their tens of thousands to the inviting green coast of Cowal. It was an open playground close enough to the heart of the industrial wasteland for them to regard it as their own backyard; a clean, sea-washed backyard unscathed by the grimy monster that the industrial revolution had unleashed to ravage the once equally green and unspoilt Clyde Valley.

Astute entrepreneurs—like Robert Hunter of Hatton, who had thoughtfully acquired a large chunk of the coast before the steamer boom transformed the holiday habits of the workers—were waiting to welcome them. The holiday resorts of Dunoon and Rothesay were born, and they got off to a cracking start.

From the mountainous northern neck, the peninsula of Cowal is bounded in the west by the embracing arm of Loch Fyne, and in the east by Loch Long and the broad waters of the Firth of Clyde. The Isle of Bute thrusts a thumb into the crablike claws of the southern seaboard, forming the Kyles of Bute, those superbly scenic straits associated the world over with the Clyde steamer traffic.

The deeply indented southern coast strengthens the impression—fostered by the shuttling car-ferries speeding back and forth between Gourock and Dunoon—that Cowal, like Bute, is an island. The success of the new ferries in providing a swift means of direct access has obscured the attractions—at least for eccentrics tired of motorways—of the long land route from Glasgow by way of Loch Lomondside, Tarbert, Loch Long, Glen Croe and Rest and Be Thankful.

Dunoon has played host to millions of holidaymakers, but the town has not encroached upon the interior; it is an urban bridgehead on the hilly coast of Cowal. The hinterland has not greatly changed from the days when the Stewart kings hunted wild boar, and the Campbells of Loch Fyne herded their black cattle along the drove road through Hell's Glen to Lochgoilhead and the markets of the south.

Dunoon crowds around a double bay—East Bay and West Bay—divided by the headland of Castle Hill. Only a few scattered stones mark the site of the historic fortress, devastated by the rampaging Murray of Atholl in 1685. The landmark on Castle Hill is the bronze statue of Robert Burns' Highland Mary, who was born near Dunoon on the site of what is now Auchamore Farm. The hapless Mary Campbell could never have foreseen that her lover's fame—and their brief liaison—would be commemorated by a statue of her crowning Castle Hill 110 years after her death.

The famous pier on the point was built by the famous Stevensons—father and uncle of the immortal Robert Louis—and its period character has not been impaired by the later reconstructions. The pier echoes the era of the paddle steamer, as do the miles of broad promenade flanked by solid Victorian villas, once the home of wealthy Glasgow merchants who had attained the supreme status symbol of a

Dunoon, Cowal and Bute

residence on the coast. The villas are now private hotels and guest houses, as unequivocally Scottish as the sustaining high teas served within their substantial walls.

Piping enthusiasts the world over have the last Friday and Saturday of August circled in their diaries. On those two day the Cowal Highland Gathering assembles in the Dunoon Sports Stadium. It is a uniquely Scottish carnival, involving the entire town and a vast influx of visitors. There are athletics, and the traditional Highland Games events such as tossing the caber, throwing the hammer and putting the shot, but the Cowal Gathering is famed as the venue where Pipe Bands compete for the coveted Argyll Shield. Entrants come from the United States, Australia, New Zealand, and even such unlikely piping centres as Sweden and the Netherlands.

The scenes at the close of the Gathering are laden with nostalgia. The massed Pipe Bands—more than a thousand strong—march back from the Sports Stadium into the town bearing their trophies through the crowded streets. Fathers hoist their sons shoulder high for a better view, just as they were once lifted on high to see the march past of the kilted giants. And for the annual thousands new to the Cowal Gathering, the spectacle of the massed pipe bands is one that will live long in their memory.

From slumbering Sandbank, birthplace—in the days of its glory before the Holy Loch became a Polaris base—of the famous racing yachts *Sceptre* and *Sovereign,* the road veers inland through Glen Lean. It switchbacks round Loch Striven to Colintraive on the tranquil shores of the Kyles of Bute. A car-ferry takes only minutes to cross the narrows to Rhubodach on the Isle of Bute.

People invariably talk of going to Rothesay, hardly ever of going to the Isle of Bute. Yet Bute is an island of enormous charm, all the greater because of the contrast with urban Rothesay.

Bute's well kept small farms, many of them planted with shelter belts of ash, sycamore and lime trees, present a picture of ordered rural serenity against the backdrop of the wild Arran hills. And there are architectural treasures such as the beautiful Norman arch in the ruined twelfth-century St Blane's Chapel, and astonishing artefacts to explore, like Thom's Cuts, an ingenious system of water cuts devised by Robert Thom in the early nineteenth century to bring more water to Loch Fad, source of power for Bute's cotton mills.

Rothesay of the vaunted bay has been renowned for centuries for its sheltered harbour. It has all the fun of a seaside resort and the attraction of a working fishing port. Visitors by train embark for Rothesay from Wemyss Bay Station, one of the glories of Victorian architecture; a fabulous creation of delicate cast-iron and glass, with a magnificent curving canopy extending down to the pierhead. Wemyss Bay is a fitting prelude to the Isle of Bute.

A set of footprints cut into an outcrop of rock beside the ruined Chapel of Keil are reputed to mark the spot where the newly exiled Columba first stood and gazed out across the North Channel, saw that his homeland was still in sight, and promptly took off again by coracle to make a fresh landfall on distant Iona. As history, the story has the authentic hollow ring of traditional guide book fantasy, laced with a little Irish whimsy. But the mixture is easily swallowed at the tip of Kintyre, with the coast of Ireland a mere twelve miles away.

Kintyre is the longest peninsula in Scotland, thrusting south-west like a great longship seeking the haven of the blue hills of Antrim. Scottish history sparked to life here. This is Dalriada, first Kingdom of the Scots.

Modern Campbeltown, standing on the site of the ancient capital of Dalruadhain, retains an aura of its regal past. The imperious sweep of its broad bay was destined for more than the presence of a fishing port and small market town. But Campbeltown—intimately linked with the countryside of Kintyre—needs no capital status to be conscious of the importance of its role. Within the sea-girt boundaries of the peninsula, Campbeltown is king. No small town in all Scotland inspires fiercer loyalties. Expatriate Campbeltonians, no matter how spectacular their success in the wider world, rarely lose touch with the town of their birth, and it seems to be the ambition of all exiles to return.

There is much to attract them. Across from Campbeltown, on the west coast, lies Machrihanish, known to golfers the world over. Few courses can claim Atlantic washed links and a neighbouring airport.

For motorists and walkers alike, one of the joys of Kintyre's coast roads is the seascapes, seen at their exhilarating best in storm, with the great Atlantic rollers crashing on the shore. The sea—richly patterned by islands—is rarely out of sight. On the west, the clustering tail of the Southern Hebrides—tiny Gigha, unlikely harbourer of the luxuriant oasis of Achamore Garden; Jura of the jutting Paps, and the Green Isle of Islay.

The east coast road, running along the length of Kilbrannan Sound, opens new windows on the majestic mountains of Arran, authentically Highland in their grandeur. The little fishing village of Carradale, surrounded by wooded glens, is tantalisingly close to the Arran hills, and the summer car ferry at Claonaig can whisk visitors across to the island.

Tarbert links Knapdale and Kintyre on the wrist-thin isthmus between the long sea loch of West Loch Tarbert and the inlet of East Loch Tarbert on Loch Fyne. Tarbert contrives to fit a workaday fishing village into an idyllic picture-postcard frame, and its harbour provides one of the safest yachting anchorages in the west.

In the eighteenth century plans were mooted for a canal across the narrow isthmus to eliminate the long sail around the Mull of Kintyre to the Atlantic Ocean. But Sir John Rennie's design for a canal linking Loch Gilp and Loch Crinan gained favour, and the nine miles long Crinan Canal was opened to shipping in 1801.

The Crinan Canal is one of the treasures of Mid Argyll; a rare instance of the works of man achieving a perfect accord with nature. In 1847, Queen Victoria made a royal progression through the canal on her way to the Western Isles. Had the monarch known the ferocious weather that awaited her in the Minch she would doubtless have made a smart about-turn at Crinan. But there were no more Hebridean cruises, and

Mid Argyll, Kintyre and Islay

Balmoral became the safely landlocked Highland seat of the Royal Family.

The Queen's sumptuously decorated barge was drawn by three horses, guided by postillions arrayed in scarlet. Such glories are no more. Nowadays, the canal is used by the Loch Fyne fishing fleet taking mundane passage to the northern fishing grounds. But faint echoes of Victoria's majestic progress are aroused when lissom thoroughbreds of yachts ease their sleek flanks through the fifteen locks.

At Crinan, on the Sound of Jura, the sea is carpeted with islands. Crinan looks out on the Dorus Mor—the Great Door—between Craignish Point and the island of Garbh Reisa. This is the sea gateway to the Hebrides; a gateway guarded by the roaring whirlpool of Corryvrechan.

The Gulf of Corryvrechan lies between the islands of Jura and Scarba. The flood tide storms west through the Gulf at a furious nine knots, smashing against underwater peaks. The upsurge creates a fearsome whirlpool, which has been the graveyard of countless vessels over the centuries. When a westerly gale challenges the tide-race the roar of the whirlpool can be heard on the Knapdale coast.

Inveraray, at the head of Loch Fyne, is the historic seat of the Chiefs of Clan Campbell. Something of the role the Campbell grandees played in Scottish history can be gathered from the titles held by Ian, the eleventh Duke of Argyll, and current holder of the title. This young man is Lord of Inveraray, Marquess of the Great Seal of Scotland, Admiral of the Western Coasts and Isles, Hereditary Sheriff of Argyll and Keeper of the Royal Castles of Dunoon, Dunstaffnage, Tarbert and Carrick.

The present Duke's ancestor, Archibald—third Duke of Argyll and Lord Justice General of Scotland—celebrated his succession to the title by initiating a building bonanza. He engaged the London architect Roger Morris—with William Adam as his assistant—to construct a palatial new castle. Dr. Johnson's comment, when he viewed the Campbell palace with Boswell, was: 'What I admire here is the total defiance of expense.'

Duke Archibald was not a man to count the coppers. As the rude huts of his clansmen impaired the landscaping of the castle grounds, Archibald conceived a truly eighteenth century ducal solution: he would lay out a new town.

By virtue of imaginative restoration work, the town of Inverary remains an elegant example of eighteenth century town planning. But Duke Archibald's Gothic castle has been less fortunate, being plagued by a series of fires, the last—and most serious—happening in November 1975.

Of all Kintyre's clustering flotilla of islands tiny Gigha is the closest to the mainland, only three miles from Tayinloan. The late Sir James Horlick's Achamore Garden is a catalogue of colour: flame trees, glowing orange-scarlet; the pinks, reds and whites of the azaleas; the Rhododendron Falconeri bearing huge creamy yellow tresses.

Islay, the most southerly of the Inner Hebrides, is one of the world's major wintering resorts of the Barnacle Goose, their annual influx far outnumbering the human population of the island. There is a fantastic variety of bird habitat—woodland, moor, hill, sea cliff, machair, sand dune, agricultural land, river, marsh, freshwater loch and the sea lochs of Indaal and Gruinart. Little wonder that so many birds favour Islay.

Oban is the natural capital of the West Highlands; a town graced by physical endowments which match the splendour of its hinterland. Bathed in the unmistakable ambience of the Gaelic west, there is an easy-going atmosphere more akin to the gentle pace of life in the islands than a mainland town. Perhaps it is the air, carrying the salt-laden tang of the isles. The weary traveller, disgorged from the overnight Glasgow train in the bleak abyss between night and morning, notices it at once. Even at that dread hour, a walk along the Esplanade is a refreshment to the senses.

One of Oban's delights is its splendidly Victorian frontages, only minimally infiltrated by the plastic fronts of the multiples. But it is not that superb Esplanade, the regal solidity of those handsome Victorian hotels lining the seafront, or the three piers and their attendant steamers, car-ferries, sturdy fishing boats, sleek yachts and scurrying motor launches that catch and hold the eye in spellbound fascination: it is the sight of a vast, roofless round tower, with a two-tiered fretwork of high pointed windows—an incredible 94 in all—squatting 230 feet above the harbour on Battery Hill, like a gigantic, stranded flying saucer from another planet.

The McCaig Tower—the brainstorm of John Stuart McCaig, born in 1824 on the island of Lismore—is the most grandiose, ludicrous and utterly marvellous Folly ever conceived by a banker. He started building in 1897 with the altruistic aim of providing work for unemployed masons, although the practical element soon gave way to his private fantasies. The banker, who never married, proposed to erect around the parapet of the Tower statues of his entire family—father and mother,

brothers and sisters—and, of course, himself. Unfortunately, he died on June 29, 1902 before this unique embellishment could be realised. Not surprisingly, the work died with him. A memorial tablet over the entrance to the Tower bears the mark of the master's hand: *Erected in 1900 by John Stuart McCaig, Art Critic and Philosophical Essayist and Banker, Oban.*

Alas, they don't make bankers like John Stuart McCaig any more, not even in Oban.

Most city fathers, lumbered with such an unfinished colossus would have had traumas or resorted to explosives. Not Oban's enlightened administrators. The interior of the roofless round tower has been imaginatively converted into a garden, and an unsung genius hit upon the notion of having the exterior floodlit. It is an act of pure theatre, magically transforming the granite monster into an ethereal delight.

There is another bonus from McCaig's lasting legacy to the town. The curious—and the incredulous—are impelled up Battery Hill for a closer look. They are well rewarded for their exertions. The seaward window arches of the round tower offer a stunning panorama—the full sweep of Oban Bay, shielded by the protective arm of Kerrera, the island of Lismore, the mainland hills of Morvern, and the looming bulk of the Isle of Mull across the Firth of Lorn.

Mull of the mountains, moors, lochs, forested glens and towering sea cliffs was cruelly shorn of its people in the last century, and that forced exodus—by an equally cruel irony of history—is one of the reasons why the island exerts such a potent spell upon the holidaymaker today. Empty beaches, deserted glens and silent hills spell space and freedom

Oban, Mull and District

to the city dweller—and Mull has space and freedom galore.

The island's capital, tiny Tobermory, its miniature main street bounded by the harbour wall, looks out upon a landlocked bay under circling hills. Tobermory is the mecca of every yachtsman in the west.

Even tinier Fionnphort—the end of the road on the long Ross of Mull—looks across the Sound of Iona to the famous grey Abbey below the green sugar lump of Dun I. Pilgrims have been ferried across the Sound for centuries, although the modern pilgrim is more likely to be carrying camera and light meter than a staff. The abbey is approached along the Street of the Dead, the ancient burial route of Scottish kings. Both MacBeth and Duncan were borne this way on their last journey. But the essence of the peace of Iona is to be found off the well trodden tourist trail in the sandy little bays on the west coast.

The austere columnar basalt pillars of Staffa rear from the sea north of Iona. Staffa and its unique caves—Fingal's Cave inspired Mendelssohn's overture *The Hebrides*—drew a galaxy of illustrious visitors in the past. Wordsworth—who moaned, in appalling verse, about 'the motley crowd' too 'volatile and loud', who had spoiled his contemplation of the scene in 1833—Keats, Sir Walter Scott, and Queen Victoria with the faithful Albert in tow. A new 47-passenger vessel *'The Laird of Staffa'* operates from Ulva Ferry in Mull, enabling the present day traveller to experience the wonders of this cavern riddled rocky outpost.

Ben Cruachan is the hollow mountain; curiously enough an accurate tag for this massive bastion of Mid Lorn. An enormous cavern—big enough to swallow Coventry Cathedral with ease—has been hacked out of Cruachan's heart. Its incumbents: four giant turbine/generating sets.

The generating turbines are reversible, and can pump the waters of Loch Awe 1200 feet up the mountain to the south corrie, where a dam 1000 feet long and 150 feet high forms a reservoir.

Driving out of the heart of the mountain—uneasily conscious of the weight of rock above—the visitor will see few sights more satisfying than the sparkling waters of Loch Awe framed in the tunnel mouth.

The Oban road thrusts through the historic Pass of Brander by way of the little village of Taynuilt at the foot of Glen Nant. It was here at Bonawe on Airds Bay, close to the mouth of the River Awe, that Richard Ford of the Newland Company of Coniston founded the Lorn Furnace in 1753, the first successful iron works in Scotland.

The Bonawe Narrows, where the upper reach of Loch Etive takes a dramatic change of course into the mountains, had always been an important communications point. The drove roads from the north converged on the Benderloch shore, the only suitable crossing place for cattle bound for the great marts in the south. But the attraction for the furnacemen was the thickly wooded countryside. They came to control 34 square miles of timber-producing land, and the furnace, employing 600 men, flourished for 120 years.

Iron ore was imported from Cumberland by three-masted sailing ships, and landed at Kelly's Pier, named after an Irish manager. Water, ingeniously flumed off the River Awe, drove the great iron water wheel which powered two large pairs of bellows, providing a continuous blast to the furnace. The old Furnace of Lorn with its bell tower—rung at 6 am and 6 pm to sound the beginning and end of the working day—still stands on the shore of Loch Etive.

The Great Herdsman of Etive—Buachaille Etive Mor of the soaring crags—keeps watch over the desolate reaches of Rannoch Moor and the Black Mount at the mouth of Glencoe. From the head of the glen, below a flat-topped rock—known in Gaelic as Innean a' Cheathaich, the Anvil of the Mist—the river Coe plunges through a gorge under a high waterfall of the Allt Lairig Eilde. Precipitous rock faces surround the pass—a circling shield of gaunt peaks, pierced by bleak ravines—spectral, eerily doom-laden in mist and rain; clothed in sombre majesty after snow.

At five o'clock on the morning of 13 February 1692, in the still aftermath of a blizzard, the most infamous massacre in Scotland's savage history took place in this glen. Unsuspecting clansmen—the MacDonalds of Glencoe, who had a company of Argyll's regiment, under the command of Captain Robert Campbell of Glenlyon, billeted on them—were attacked by the soldiers they were sheltering.

'This is by the King's special command,' Captain Campbell's written instructions carefully pointed out, 'and for the good and safety of the country, that those miscreants be cutt off root and branch.'

The fate of a small Highland clan, widely regarded as robbers and cattle thieves, would have evoked little sympathy had the manner of the killing been different. But even seventeenth century brigands, weaned on ferocious blood feuds that were pursued to the death for generations, had their own code of honour. The killing of the MacDonalds by the Campbells was seen as murder under trust, the most abhorrent crime of all. The Campbell name was execrated, and the deed never forgotten.

Captain Campbell had been ordered to 'putt all to the sword under seventy.' But some of the old chief's clansmen escaped in the snow, and struggled through the high passes to the safety of Appin. Those pitiful survivors of the massacre could have never foreseen that a day would come when their snow-clad mountains would provide an escape of a vastly different kind.

The north easterly face of Meall a' Rhuiridh—which holds snow long after it has melted from other slopes—has some of the finest ski-ing runs in Scotland, offering racing 'pistes' for the expert and gentle slopes for the novice. Access could hardly be easier. The old Glencoe road has been extended beyond Black Rock Cottage to a chalet, which is the starting point of a chair-lift up to 2100 feet. Beyond the chair-lift terminal, T-bar tows whisk skiers up the remaining 1250 feet, depositing them on the summit with their energies unimpaired.

After an active day on the heights, skiers—and Glencoe's ever-present rock climbers and hill walkers—can relax in one of Scotland's oldest hostelries, the Kingshouse Inn.

For those to whom a Highland journey is incomplete without a ferry crossing, there is the Corran ferry plying across Loch Linnhe to Ardgour and the most island-like of all Highland peninsulas, Ardnamurchan—the Point of the Great Ocean.

Once down the ferry ramp, take the road through Glen Tarbert to the village of Strontian, snugly ensconced on a sheltered inlet of Loch Sunart, an unlikely locale for industrial activity. But Strontian was famous for its lead mines, which flourished from the early eighteenth century to the start of the twentieth.

In 1968, the Scottish Office announced that Strontian was to be the

Fort William and District

rst Highland village to be given a facelift as part of a planned redevelopment. The new housing, and an imaginative central complex—shop, tearoom, old people's home, school—contrive to retain the character of the old village whilst providing a visually stimulating focal point for the new. Strontian is a splendid example of what can be achieved by really imaginative planning and design.

Follow the road along the shores of Loch Sunart through Glen Borrodale; climb above the horse-shoe bay of Camus na Gael, and strike inland across the empty moorland to Kilchoan of the sweeping bay. In late Spring, rhododendrons flame in the Borrodale woods, purple heathrift colours the rocks and wild yellow iris bloom along the shore.

On the Point of Ardnamurchan, 23 miles further west than Land's End, the lighthouse commands the most spectacular seascape in Scotland. By courtesy of the Head Keeper, you can climb the 140 stone steps inside the tower, and the two ladders up to the Lamp House. Any breath you have left will be taken by the fantastic spread of islands across the western sea: Tiree, Coll, Muck, the great beak of the Scuirr of Eigg, the vast hulk of Rhum, Staffa, Iona, the mighty ramparts of the Cuillins in Skye, and the long chain of Outer Isles from Barra to the Butt of Lewis.

What better way to leave the peace of Ardnamurchan—encapsulated in Sanna Bay with its vast stretches of white shell-sand and sheltering dunes—than by the magnificent new highway that sweeps regally from Kinlochmoidart to Lochailort.

Fort William has developed from a strategically sited military encampment at the southern pivot of the Great Glen into the principal industrial, commercial and holiday centre of Lochaber. The town's narrow High Street is the unlikely springboard to country of a wild magnificence. Glen Nevis is no more than a mile away; a mild foretaste to the spectacle of the mighty Mamore range—an ocean of rock rising in crested wave upon wave under the massive flank of Ben Nevis. Add the lochs and glens of Eil, Arkaig and Garry—and a man-made wonder, the Mallaig Extension, 41¾ miles of the greatest scenic railway in Britain.

Crossing Telford's Caledonian Canal by swing bridge—pivoted on one bank to leave the channel clear for shipping—the railway line passes under the shoulder of the great Ben and follows the shore of Loch Eil, buttressed by 17 sea walls. Climbing into the enclosing hills, it bursts into the open soaring over the vast bowl of the glen at the head of Loch Shiel on a curving white viaduct of 21 pillared arches 100 feet high.

Passengers can see below the Glenfinnan Tower Monument marking the spot where Prince Charles Edward Stuart unfurled his standard on that grey Monday morning of 19 August 1745. The Young Pretender eschewed the tartan. He wore 'a red-laced west coat and breeches and a dun coat with a yellow bob at his Hat.'

By Loch Eilt, by Loch Ailort, by little Loch Dubh, by Loch nan Uamh, by Arisaig and Morar of the delectable sands the line threads its way—'floated' on brushwood over peat bogs, lifted on viaducts across rivers and glens, thrust through rock cuttings and tunnels—to the Sound of Sleat, and the clamouring gulls of Mallaig announcing journey's end.

This heroic feat of engineering was the work of 'Concrete Bob' McAlpine and his army of anonymous navvies. Salute them by abandoning your car, and taking a ride on their line.

26 The natural assets of Speyside are legion. Flanked by the Monadhliadh—the Grey Mountains—and the vast massif of the Cairngorms, the long Valley of the Spey affords an ideal location for all manner and kind of active recreation all the year round.

The Cairngorms are the highest mountain range in Britain; Ben Macdhui, at 4,296 feet, only just managing to rise above the clustering peaks of his giant near neighbours. With their semi-permanent snow-fields, beguilingly remote corries, high tundras, alpine flora and elusive wildlife, the high tops of the Cairngorms have a wilderness beauty and lonely splendour that is peculiarly their own.

The River Spey reigns supreme in the valley, world renowned for its salmon. But there are other rivers—and a variety of lochs—to lure the angler; exhilarating snow slopes to test the reflexes of the most experienced skier, with expert coaching available on nursery slopes for young—and old—beginners; camping sites on the alpine shores of Loch Morlich—more than 1,000 feet above sea level—to enhance the joys of life under canvas; and a multitude of glens and straths free of intrusion from all but the hillwalker, or the pony trekker mounted on a sure-footed Highland garron.

Pony-trekking was pioneered in the holiday village of Newtonmore. There is an alpine air about Newtonmore, 800 feet above sea level in the birch and pine fringed strath of the Upper Spey. Stirring battles still take place on the green of The Eilan—the playing field below Creag Dubh—scene of many of the triumphs of the Newtonmore Camanachd Club, for decades the premier shinty team in the Highlands.

The eighteenth century Duke of Gordon's plans to convert the old village of Kingussie into a major centre of the woollen industry never materialised, but the village has become the quiet capital and principal shopping centre of Badenoch. Kingussie's Highland Folk Museum—Am Fasgadh—under the care of four Scottish universities opens a window on the old Highland way of life.

Clive Freshwater's Canoeing and Sailing School at Loch Insh has succeeded in maintaining ancient navigational rights on the River Spey, a freedom landed proprietors sought to usurp. The Loch Insh School provides expert tuition in dinghy sailing and canoeing. An expedition by canoe on the Spey is one of the most rewarding ways of exploring the valley.

Midway between Kingussie and Aviemore, there is a newcomer to the Speyside scene, the 260-acre Highland Wildlife Park. The aim of the Wildlife Park is to bring back extinct species that once roamed the forests. Among the many animals restored to their former habitat are the wild boar, lynx, bear, polecat and wolf.

The Aviemore Centre consists of a complex of hotels and a motel with 'Swiss-style' chalets, accommodating more than 1,000 guests; a theatre/cinema seating 720; exhibition halls; conference and banqueting suites; a heated indoor swimming pool; an ice-skating and curling rink; a wide range of restaurants, grill rooms and snack bars; Kart racing track; children's playrooms; shops, and a hairdressing salon. The latest addition to this self-contained holiday village conceived by the late Lord Fraser of Allander is a Santa Claus Land, complete with a perpetual Claus and a permafrost 'North Pole', the latter by courtesy of Messrs Walls Ice Cream.

Spey Valley

Aviemore has become synonomous with winter sports in Scotland. The middle station of the Chairlift links up with the White Lady Shieling where hot drinks and snacks are dispensed, and a restaurant on the upper floor caters for the needs of those made ravenous by the invigorating air. Perched beside the top terminal, the Ptarmigan Restaurant is an impertinent pimple on the majestic brow of Cairngorm, but at 3,600 feet it can claim to be the highest restaurant in Britain.

The Osprey Hide at Loch Garten has little in common with the trendy unisex gear and raffish dark glasses of the hotching ski slopes. Silence and stillness reap a rich reward here, enabling the watcher to study those aloof aristocrats of the air the great fish-eating hawks. Ospreys are in supreme command of their element, and to see them in lazy gliding flight is to witness a poetic arabesque in the air. Lucky watchers may see the cock bird hovering over the nest with a fresh-caught trout in his talons. Or observe the young engaging in vigorous wing exercises prior to launching themselves into the air for the first time.

Landmark, at Carrbridge, is the first Visitor Centre in Europe. The multi-screen auditorium—with stereo sound equipment—projects the story of Man in the Highlands from the last Ice Age to the present day, and the environmental exhibition adds an imaginative new dimension to an understanding of Highland history.

Not least among the thoughtful innovations provided by *Landmark* is its car park and picnic area, ingeniously dispersed among a stand of tall pines, and the tasteful simplicity of its excellent restaurant, the walls decorated with a stunning collection of blown-up photographs of life in the area in late Victorian and early Edwardian times. Even the wine list folder is employed to extend the knowledge of the visitor, containing information on twenty-three local malt whiskies, the covers illustrated with a rare photograph, almost a century old, of an illicit still watched over by two barefoot Highland urchins, and a map locating Speyside distilleries.

Landmark has set new standards in the tourist field by showing an imaginative regard for Highland history, and a respect for the intelligence of visitors.

On the fourth of September 1860, Queen Victoria — travelling incognito—spent a night in Grantown-on-Spey after a strenuous pony-trekking expedition from Balmoral by way of Glen Feshie. The energetic royal sightseer had her party out of the Grant Arms Hotel early in the morning for a quick sortie by coach to Castle Grant, the seat of Lord Seafield. The Queen was not impressed. 'A very plain-looking house, like a factory,' she confided to her Journal, adding caustically, 'We did not get out.'

Few travellers today—even if they were not attending the Scottish Norwegian Ski School—would fail to get out at Grantown-on-Spey. The capital of Strathspey has a style and grace worthy of its setting.

Nine miles from Aviemore at the summit of the Lairig Ghru—the highest pass in Britain—the hill walker has an eagle's eye view of Speyside. It is a view that never palls—spring, summer, autumn or winter—and those who have once climbed up through the Rothiemurchus forest to the pass are drawn irresistibly back again.

Inverness is one of the oldest inhabited localities in Scotland. Men hunted and fished here centuries before the first Christian missionaries brought word of the new religion. King Brude ruled his Pictish kingdom from a palisaded fort beside the River Ness, and the early Scots monarchs made frequent forays to the town whenever the Highland chieftains looked like upstaging them.

Inverness was proclaimed a Royal Burgh in the twelfth century by King David I, who crowned Castlehill with its first stone keep. From its commanding eminence above the River Ness a royal fortress watched over the northern and western approaches for six hundred years.

On September 22, 1563, Mary Queen of Scots was refused entry to the castle by Alexander Gordon, acting a trifle precipitately on behalf of his rebel chief the Earl of Huntly. This rash stroke of lese-majesty met with swift and merciless retribution. Nine days later the castle was stormed. Alexander Gordon and five of his henchmen were hanged from the walls as rebels taken in arms against the Queen.

The town was occupied by Cromwell's Commonwealth forces in November 1651. Three centuries before the Pentagon was as much as a gleam in the eye of an American military planner, Major-General Deane started work on a gigantic Citadel of pentagon shape. The west wall fronted the River Ness, and the other four sides were surrounded by a wide fosse. Fed from the river at high tide, the fosse had sufficient depth of water to float a barque. The breastworks of the Citadel were three storeys high; the main entrance defended by a drawbridge of heavy oak timbers.

Cromwell's Pentagon, which took five years to complete, garrisoned 1000 men and 160 horse. Regarded by military experts as impregnable, the mighty Citadel was razed to the ground on the restoration of Charles II.

Another military occupation — that of the Jacobites in the Forty-Five Rising — ended the reign of the old castle on the hill. Reconstructed by the Hanoverian Government, the castle had become known as Fort George, a name unlikely to appeal to Bonnie Prince Charlie, who ordered its destruction. The demolition was executed with typical Jacobite ineptitude.

The French sergeant of artillery in charge thought that one of the fuses had gone out. He ran to relight the fuse, his dog at his heels. There was an almighty explosion. Man and dog were blown clean across the River Ness. The dog survived, but the French sergeant perished with the castle.

In the aftermath of Culloden, a new Fort George of vast dimension was built at Ardersier. The present baronial edifice on Castlehill made its appearance in the first half of the nineteenth century and serves as a Sheriff Court House.

Little remains of the old town that once huddled under the walls of the castle on the hill. The red sandstone houses with stepped gables and turnpike stairs — the upper galleries hanging so low over the narrow streets that the dragoons of Butcher Cumberland's Guard had to crouch over the manes of their horses as they rode by — are no more. But Cumberland's dragoons would recognise the river, still cutting a broad swathe through the town on its sweep to the sea.

An impressive newcomer has appeared on the banks of the Ness —

Inverness, Loch Ness and Nairn

the Eden Court Theatre. Opened in April 1976, the theatre complex is the most exhilarating development ever undertaken by a local authority in Scotland. Eden Court's angled, steeply pitched slated roofs cluster around the high-walled auditorium in a curiously satisfying amity with the old ecclesiastical Palace of Bishop Eden, which has been imaginatively incorporated in the theatre complex, and adapted for offices, dressing rooms and exhibition centre.

Diners in the riverside restaurant look out on the tree-lined Ness flowing past Castlehill. The 814-seat auditorium is a brilliant concept, its circling three tiers of boxes creating a sense of intimate contact with the performers on stage. Ballet, opera, symphony and pop concerts, drama and folk festivals have all been presented in the theatre by the river. Eden Court also functions as Scotland's fifth regional film theatre, and the work of some of the cinema's most significant directors has been shown.

Although it caused the indomitable Thomas Telford many a headache, the Caledonian Canal affords the perfect retreat from the hustle and tension of the roads. The Clachnaharry Lock — the biggest in the world at the time of its construction — at the entrance to the canal is only a hop, skip and jump away from one of the busiest sections of the A9. But it marks the start of the great divide. On the road, a snarl of traffic: on the green banks of the waterway, a serene quiet.

Take a cruise down the canal past sturdy little Bona Light into the vast reach of that most famous of all lochs — Loch Ness. The loch covers an area of 22 square miles, and the sheer volume of water is overpowering, almost forbidding. Old Castle Urquhart watches over waters deeper than the North Sea.

Well publicised hunts for the 'monster' — Sir Peter Scott's 'Nessitera Rhombopteryx' has not caught on — by midget submarine, tungsten TV lamps, strobe lights, time-lapse cameras, SX-70 Polaroids, and all manner of sophisticated underwater devices have revealed more about human behaviour than the mysterious denizen of the loch. The improbably named Dr. Zug, curator of amphibians and reptiles at the Smithsonian Institute in Washington, has declared, "I am not going to identify the thing until I meet it eye to eye." The form book does not suggest an early eyeball to eyeball confrontation for the good Dr. Zug. But enthusiasts continually scour Loch Ness from Foyers — the unlikely birthplace in 1894 of Britain's first industrial hydro-electric power station and aluminium smelter — to Fort Augustus, named in honour of Augustus, the dread Duke of Cumberland.

There is no better memorial to Victorian technology than the railway viaduct spanning the Nairn river at Culloden. Built entirely of red sandstone, the 1800-ft long viaduct rises on 29 high arches. It is a lasting monument to Murdo Paterson, chief engineer of the old Highland Railway who died at the stationmaster's house on Culloden Moor when supervising the building of his great viaduct.

Sand, sea and a sparkling clarity of light characterise Nairn. It is a short trip from Telford's long harbour mole through the immensely fertile coastal plain to Cawdor of the superbly preserved Castle and noble trees. And beyond snug Cawdor there are the isolated farmsteads, high moorland and wild hinterland of Findhorn.

Situated in a lush green bowl, Strathpeffer contrives to be at one with its environment, whilst displaying Victorian holiday architecture at its most exuberantly confident. The Highland Hotel presides over The Square—a tree-ringed concourse at the heart of the resort—like a gigantic cricket pavilion, its pagoda-like twin towers rising high above a long, colonnaded balcony. The Highland is matched by the aptly named Ben Wyvis, conceived on the grand scale, with landscaped grounds and curving drive of proportions deemed fitting to grace such a leviathan. On the terraced slopes, Victorian mansions and villas—discreetly clothed in a profusion of trees, shrubs and flowers—vie with one another in size and singularity.

One of Scotland's few Spas, Strathpeffer's popularity was at its height in the late nineteenth century. Famed for the healing properties of its sulphur and chalybeate springs, English gentry, European nobility and American industrial barons headed the ranks of the well-heeled who flocked to take the waters.

A restored Pump Room still stands, dwarfed by the Spa Pavilion. Not the original Pavilion where the Victorians enjoyed 'spacious accommodation for balls, concerts and refreshments', but an equally spacious successor, where eight hundred dancers regularly take the floor. The Golf Course on Ulladale Hill has acquired a new Club House, decked with a weather-vane topped cupola. But the view from the first tee along the verdant valley remains unchanged, and the Club offers an additional attraction—a tiny fishing loch, stocked with brown trout.

Castle Leod, ancestral seat of the Earl of Cromarty, stands less than a mile north of Strathpeffer. A Tower House, built in 1616, Castle Leod

must rank as the homeliest and most attractive little castle in Scotland. On the first Saturday in August the Castle grounds become the setting of the Strathpeffer Highland Games, a role for which they might have been artfully designed.

Another ancestral seat is Foulis Castle, near Evanton, home of the Chiefs of the martial Clan Munro. General Sir Hector Munro—scourge of Suraja Dowla and the Indian rebels; hero of the relief of Negapatam—ensured that his military exploits would never be totally eclipsed from public view. In 1782, this military egomaniac employed local stonemasons to construct a replica of the Gates of Negapatam on Fyrish Hill above the village of Evanton. This bizarre memento of Sir Hector's triumph in the long-forgotten Indian campaign warrants a bicentary celebration in 1982—of the enduring skills of the anonymous stonemasons.

Dingwall—road and rail junction, and the old county town—derives its name from its eleventh century Norse colonisers who called the settlement 'Thing vollr', the Place of Meeting. The natural centre of the fertile agricultural lands of Easter Ross, Dingwall has retained its identity as a market town. The only invasions today are those by friendly farmers and their store sheep and cattle which pass through the auction marts in great numbers.

Controversy breaks out from time to time as to how such a verdant peninsula as the Black Isle—a green and pleasant land, hedgerows thick with willow herbs and forget-me-nots, fields bright with corn marigolds, hillsides ablaze with gaudy splashes of colour from broom and whin—acquired such an incongruous name. The Black Isle is

Easter Ross and Black Isle

ranslation of the Gaelic An t-Eilean Dubh; an accurate description when he name was originally given. The Old Statistical Account confirms that p to the eighteenth century the peninsula was mostly uncultivated lack moorland. As for 'Isle', in Gaelic the same word serves for both sland' and 'peninsula'.

Under its old, more mellifluous name of Ardmeanach, the lordship of he Black Isle was the gift of Mary Queen of Scots. Never noted for her udgement, she bestowed it on Darnley. He was not the only doom-aden figure to have featured in the long history of the Black Isle.

The ancient walls of Fortrose Cathedral witnessed the trial of Coin-each Odhar, the Brahan Seer, whose apocalyptic prophecies—or Alexander MacKenzie's version of them—are still widely read in the Highlands. Found guilty of witchcraft, his devout judges were merciless. A stone at Chanonry Point marks the spot where the incautious Coin-each was upended into a spiked barrel of boiling pitch.

The waters off Fortrose once sheltered Admiral Byng's Navy, gath-red to protect the flank of the Duke of Cumberland's army as it dvanced on Culloden Moor. Nowadays, the Chanonry Sailing Club, vhose annual Regatta attracts entries from the length and breadth of Scotland, presides over the firth. Both Fortrose and neighbouring Ro-emarkie with its sheltered, sandy coves are admirable centres for a elaxed holiday, ashore or afloat.

Cromarty, on the tip of the peninsula where the North and South Sutars guard the entrance to the Cromarty Firth, was a boom town at the tart of the nineteenth century. A bustling centre of the coastal trade, the harbour teemed with sloops bound for ports around the Scottish coast and the continent. Hemp, flax and flour mills flourished in the town.

The legacy of those days can be seen in the handsome three-storeyed town houses of the merchants, which give Cromarty such a period flavour. But the coming of the railways sounded the death-knell of the coastal shipping trade. Cromarty languished, seemingly doomed to decline. By one of those curious quirks of history, its off-the-beaten-track isolation from the main traffic throughways, which threatened to make Cromarty a ghost town, seem likely to prove its salvation as quiet retreats of an individual character become increasingly valued.

Manufacturing industry has crossed to the north shore of the Firth. Invergordon houses a gleaming aluminium smelter, one of the most advanced in Europe. Along the coast at Nigg, the first steel oil platform jacket to be constructed in the Highlands was floated out of its vast graving dock in August 1974, and towed through the Sutars to the Forties Field.

None of the new activity has disturbed the tranquility of Tain. The Gaelic name for the town was Baile Dhubhthaich—Duthus' Town—called after its patron saint. The little ruined Chapel of St. Duthus was for long a place of pilgrimage. James V made seven pilgrimages, although the saint does not seem to have favoured him, for the penitent king died shortly after his last barefoot homage in 1513. It was the year of the fateful Battle of Flodden.

Today's pilgrims to Tain are holidaymakers. This snug little town on the Dornoch Firth, with its Tolbooth and medieval tower housing the curfew bell, offers sanctuary from the harsher world of the great cities.

31

There are historical reasons why most of the villages and crofting townships of sparsely populated Wester Ross are scattered around the deeply indented seaboard. In the early nineteenth century crofters were cleared to the shore, their hill grazings converted into sheep runs. During the later boom in sporting estates, vast tracts of land were anaesthetized for sport. Lord Middleton emptied the heart of Applecross of people. It became a sporting wilderness, strictly preserved for deer.

Isolated by urban standards, the small communities of Wester Ross have a strong sense of identity and enjoy a quality of life that is all too rare today. Everyone is known by name, often a long Gaelic patronymic, embellished by a wickedly mordant nickname—a custom dear to the heart of the Gael. It is this powerful sense of personal identity, and freedom from the corrosive pressures of urban congestion and anonymity that may account for the uniform kindliness of the people in their dealings with strangers.

Of all the routes to the incomparable west there is none better than the road from Inverness by way of Invermoriston. Beyond Cluanie Inn the road forces a way through mountain-hemmed Glen Shiel, walled by the whale-backed ridge of The Saddle and the bare rock faces of the Five Sisters of Kintail.

Where Telford's old road crossed to the south bank of the River Shiel over a narrow stone bridge there is a National Trust for Scotland sign marking the site of the Battle of Glenshiel. The battle took place on June 10, 1719—birthday of the ill-fated Old Pretender, James Francis Edward Stuart—and was the last invasion of these shores by foreign troops.

General Wightman engaged the rebels in late afternoon. By nightfall the motley Jacobite army—including several hundred Spaniards as well as followers of Scotland's most famous outlaw, Rob Roy Macgregor—had retreated up the steep slopes of the mountain that has been known ever since as Sgurr nan Spainteach, the Peak of the Spaniards. Under cover of the brief midsummer night, the Highlanders ghosted away through the dark hill passes. In the morning, the hungry Spaniards surrendered.

Three months later the Jacobites' absentee leader was enjoying a sumptuous wedding feast in Rome. His bride, Princess Clemintina Sobieski, gave birth to Prince Charles Edward the following summer. Unlike his father, the Young Pretender actually saw Glen Shiel—from a cave in the hills when he was fleeing the Redcoats after the disaster of Culloden.

The road breaks out of the confines of the glen at Shiel Bridge, rounding the head of Loch Duich and opening up memorable vistas of the long reach of Duich, the forested hillsides rising from its shores, and the surrounding mountain peaks. The new fast road to Kyle of Lochalsh keeps close to the lochside, skirting the old Kintail Shooting Lodge, now converted to an hotel. All who pass this way should salute the memory of Percy Unna.

In the old days sporting proprietors discouraged visitors to their private playgrounds, even threatening their tenants with eviction if they took in guests. Early this century a young English climber was summarily ordered off the mountains by the shooting overlord of the Kintail Estate. The climber's name was Percy Unna. In 1944 the 21,000-acre

Wester Ross

Kintail Estate, including the magnificent Five Sisters, came up for sale. The estate was bought by the now not so young but affluent Percy Unna, who gifted the land to the National Trust for Scotland. One of his conditions was that there should be free access at all times for climbers and hill-walkers.

Most visitors speed on—halted only by the fairly-tale confection of Eilean Donan Castle—to Kyle of Lochalsh. They miss one of the most delectable roads in the west. It meanders along the far shore of Loch Duich through the forestry village of Ratagan with its beautifully sited lochside youth hostel, and the little hamlet of Letterfearn, once noted for its illicit whisky stills. The road comes to a dead end—literally—at tiny Totaig, giving a new meaning to the word 'backwater'. From Totaig the almost impossible can be achieved—a fresh view of Eilean Donan and its wildly theatrical backdrop of mountains.

The Glenelg road hauls itself up to the pass of Mam Ratagan by a series of incredible hairpin bends. Breaks in the forest offer tantalising glimpses of the gleaming waters of Loch Duich far below. Near the summit the ground is clear of trees, giving an airborne view of the whole reach of the loch, with the Five Sisters of Kintail visible in all their regal magnificence, and the beckoning mountains of Skye across the western sea.

Over the top, the road rushes down the broad valley of Glenmore, cut by its tumultous river. Before entering the village of Glenelg a right fork passes the hamlet of Galder, and goes by a sandy beach round a shoulder of rocky hill to the old jetty facing across the tidal race of the Narrows to Kylerhea, the Skye junction of the old drove road.

Beyond palindrome Glenelg there is the ancient Broch of Dun Telve in Glen Beag, and the thin thread of the coast road that climbs and twists and dips its way to Sandaig, the 'Camusfearna' of Gavin Maxwell's *Ring of Bright Water*. And remote Sandaig is not the end of the road. It goes on, wheeling away from the Sound of Sleat to follow the shores of lonely Loch Hourn—alive with fishing boats two centuries ago when the loch teemed with colossal shoals of herring—to the tiny, slumbering hamlets of Camus Ban and Corran. This *is* the wild west, with the harsh peaks of Knoydart across the loch guarding a land bereft of people where the stag and his hunter are king.

Wester Ross offers a surfeit of riches. There is the high moorland of the Applecross peninsula jewelled with tiny lochans, where the Bealach na Bo, the precipitous Pass of the Cattle climbs high above Loch Kishorn, which spawned the world's biggest master oil production platform, a 400,000-ton colossus.

Torridon, with the high road to Diabaig through the Bealach na Gaoithe—the Pass of the Wind—chasing the setting sun down to the western sea.

Loch Maree of the pine-clad islands pointing the way to Gairloch of the sandy bays and Inverewe, where Osgood MacKenzie worked his magical transformation, turning a bleak, windswept peninsula into a resplendent oasis of colour. Ullapool, home of international sea angling championships, and mainland port of the Stornoway car-ferry. Dreamy Achilitibuie, and its attendant bird-haunted Summer Isles.

Wester Ross cannot be confined within a few hundred words, or its exploration to a single visit.

From Kyle of Lochalsh on the mainland shore, the car-ferries shuttle thousands of visitors across the narrow strait to the little fishing village of Kyleakin. No scene is more evocative to the Skye exile—and not only the native-born *Sgitheanach* regards absence from Skye as exile—than the tide-swept jetty beside the weather-ravaged walls of ruined Castle Maoil.

Five miles west of Kyleakin the straggling township of Breakish flanks the village of Broadford spread around its wide bay under the looming presence of Beinn na Caillich, the Hill of the Old Woman. The signpost 'Waterloo' is an alien intruder in an island of Gaelic and Norse place names. It points to a township south of Broadford, so called because of the large number of veterans of Wellington's army who once crofted the land there. The sparse soil of Skye has yielded many men to the colours — 1600 fought at the Battle of Waterloo.

Broadford is the ideal base for exploring Strathaird and Sleat. Take the road inland, skirting the Red Hills, by way of Torrin and Loch Slapin. The little crofting township of Torrin is overlooked by the pinnacled ridge of mighty Blaven, a great crested wave of rock.

The road creeps around the head of Loch Slapin and descends through Elgol to Loch Scavaig, with the incomparable range of the Cuillins girding the far shore—peak after jagged peak. Sgurr Alasdair, Alexander's Peak; at 3251 feet, the highest of them all by a short head, first climbed in 1873 by Sheriff Alexander Nicolson—a native of Skye—and named after him. Sgurr Dearg, the Red Peak; Sgurr Ghreadaidh, the Peak of Torment; Sgurr nan Gillean, the Peak of the Young Men; Sgurr Dubh, the Black Peak—and a score more.

Curiously enough, no man had a greater passion for the Cuillins than a Professor of Organic Chemistry, Norman Collie. He spent all his spare time climbing them, and died in Skye during the second world war. Norman Collie put his feelings into words as far back as 1897, and there has never been a more sensitive interpretation of the spell cast by these mountains.

The Professor of Organic Chemistry saw the striking individuality of the Cullins *'in the obscure and secret beauty born of the mists, the rain and the sunshine.'*

'Once there was a time,' he wrote, *'when these peaks were the centre of a great cataclysm; they are the shattered remains of a vast volcano that ages since poured its lavas in mighty flood far and wide over the land; since then the glaciers in prehistoric time have polished and worn down the corries and the valley floors, leaving scars and wounds everywhere as a testimony of their power; but now the fire age and the ice age are past, the still clear waters of Coruisk ripple in the breeze, by the loch-side lie the fallen masses of the hills, and the shattered debris left by the ice; these harbour the dwarf hazel, the purple heather, and the wild flowers, whilst corrie, glen, and mountain-side bask in the summer sunlight.'*

'But when the wild Atlantic storms sweep across the mountains; when the streams gather in volume, and the bare rock pinnacles, and sky, loch, and hill-side is one dull grey, the Coolin can be savage and dreary indeed; perhaps though the clouds towards the evening may break, then the torn masses of vapour, tearing in mad hunt along the ridges, will be lit up by the rays of the sun slowly descending into the western sea, and as

Skye

the light flashes from the black rocks, and the shadows deepen in the corries, the superb beauty, the melancholy, the mystery of these mountains of the Isle of Mist will be revealed.'

Sleat has a softer, more gentle face. There is a classical sylvan air about the little crofting townships dotted among the wooded grassy glades between Ardvasar and Isle Ornsay—the ebb tide island—an idyllically situated hamlet that more than matches its mellifluous name. But the Aird of Sleat where the road peters out into a track leading to the Point—the most southerly headland of Skye—presents a stark contrast. The Aird is barren, although it has magnificent compensations; superb seascapes all around, with the great hills of Knoydart, Morar, Moidart and Ardnamurchan rising in the east; the dramatic Scuir of Eigg, Rhum and Canna in the south, and the long arc of the Outer Hebrides in the west.

The road north from Broadford swings west by Loch Ainort, plunges through the hills to Sconser and Sligachan, and undulates along Glen Varragill to the capital of Skye, Portree. The distinctive flat-topped beacon of Dun Caan on the island of Raasay is rarely out of sight, and a car-ferry service from Sconser makes Raasay easily accessible.

'We saw before us a beautiful bay', wrote Jamie Boswell, recounting his visit to the island with Dr. Johnson, *'well defended, with a rocky coast; a good gentleman's house, a fine verdure about it, a considerable number of trees, and beyond it hills and mountains in graduation of wildness. Our boatmen sang with great glee.'*

The present day boatmen of Raasay have little to sing about. Sadly, the 'good gentleman's house'—Raasay House; a noble and historic building—has been allowed to fall into dereliction. But what Boswell called 'the fine verdure of Raasay' can still be savoured, and there is no finer vantage point to view Loch Sligachan and the glories of the massed peaks of the Cuillins.

Portree clusters around its land-locked harbour at the base of the matchless peninsula of Trotternish, which is bisected by the long, ridged spine of the Storr range and the Quiraing. The main road north clings to the coast nosing near Rubha Hunish—the most northerly point on the island—before dipping south through the plain of Kilmuir to Uig.

Those drawn to the weird rocks of the Quiraing and the hidden Table Rock—a smooth expanse of emerald green turf, enclosed by bare rock walls, high in the crags—can take the corkscrewing hill road from Brogaig in Staffin, which penetrates the heart of the Quiraing before crossing the high moorland and joining the Kilmuir road above Uig. From Uig of the enclosed bay the road takes a long detour by way of Loch Snizort before swinging west to Vaternish and Duirinish.

Dunvegan lies between the two peninsulas at the head of Loch Dunvegan, famed for what is reputed to be the oldest inhabited castle in the British Isles. Dunvegan Castle is known to travellers the world over, but it is doubtful if many visitors to Skye have heard of the tiny hamlet of Stein on the shore of Loch Bay in Vaternish.

Stein was founded by the British Fisheries Society in 1787. But dreams of a bustling seaport harvesting the rich fishing waters of the Minch never materialised. Something of the aura of that unrealised dream clings to this tiny settlement looking out on the western sea, although the inviting old inn is wholly free of melancholy.

The geographical apartness of the Western Isles—lying 40 miles off the northwest coast of Scotland—has been a major factor in preserving their individual identity. This splintered arc of islands—stretching 130 miles from the Butt of Lewis in the north to Barra Head in the south—represents the heartland of the *Gaidhealtachd,* the Land of the Gael, last major redoubt of the ancient Gaelic language.

Stornoway is the vigorous island capital of Lewis, compactly grouped around a beautifully landlocked harbour that penetrates the heart of the town. The town has the aura of a metropolis in miniature, but it is an urban centre with a difference. The cause is rooted in the islanders' life-style rather than such superficial differences as the bi-lingual street signs, strange though it is for those from a monoglot culture to be confronted by Church St. Sraid Na H-Eaglaise. Despite the thrusting traffic, the townsfolk have time to stop and talk; time to greet a friend with the distinctive island salute of a long, lingering handclasp; time to become immersed in the voluble, gossipy chat that is an essential part of the life of the Gaelic speaking islander.

The weekday bustle vanishes on Sunday. Take a walk through the thickly wooded castle grounds. The sea wall gate below the Lodge overlooks the Inner Harbour where the fishing fleet is at rest for the weekend.

Nothing stirs in the harbour, save the black heads of inquisitive seals. All that can be heard is the murmuring slap of the tide against the hulls of the moored fishing boats, the cry of a frustrated gull, and the slow tolling of a church bell.

Sixteen miles from Stornoway, westwards across the lochan dappled moors, the austere neolithic temple of Callanish triumphantly defies the ravages of time. Seton Gordon has recalled that the Standing Stones of Callanish were once known to the locals as *Na Fir Breige*—The False Men—a wonderfully evocative description. Viewed from a distance, some of the megaliths have an uncanny resemblance to human figures with tiny heads, like Henry Moore sculptures.

But it is when the sun goes down over Loch Roag that the brooding aura of Callanish is at its most potent. The waters of the loch seem to be creeping up on the land—land, sea and sky coalescing in one element, dominated by these shadowy figures of such awesome antiquity.

At its western apex the Callanish road threads through hillocks mottled with rock faces that the thin skin of vegetation has failed to cover, and swings through Carloway, a crofting township deeply rooted in the sparse soil of Lewis. Men and women have worked this ground for untold centuries under the commanding presence of the Broch of Dun Carloway, rising high on a steep green knoll looking out on the island speckled loch and the blue hills of Harris.

The glorious circular symmetry of the inward-sloping outer wall of the broch is a miracle of craftsmanship, wrought by a people without a written language. But the ancient stones of the fortress tower tell their own eloquent story in the quiet that enshrouds it; a quiet made the deeper by the gentle stir of the wind in the grass, the song of a lark on high, and the distant bleating of sheep.

An early traveller to the Long Island felt obliged to report the fact that Lewis and Harris are regarded as separate islands—'*which two although they ioyne be a necke of land ar accounted dyvers Ylands*'—and

Western Isles

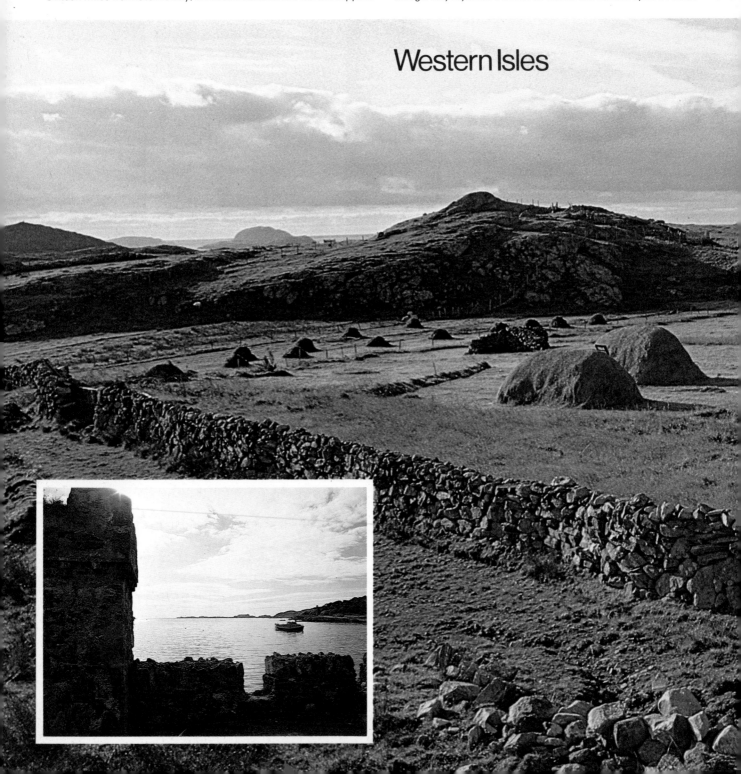

could barely conceal his astonishment. But there is a natural division to account for the separate communites; the moors and lochans of Lewis give way with dramatic suddeness to the towering mass of Clisham and her neighbouring peaks; a formidable Harris frontier barrier in the days when roads were non-existent.

The east coast of Harris is a tumbled sea of rock—a Hebridean Aden—pocked with green where crofters, who had been evicted from the fertile west to make way for sheep, once cultivated the misleadingly named lazy beds with the *cas-chrom*, a back-breaking foot plough.

At Tarbert only a narrow isthmus of land keeps the Atlantic and the Minch apart. Seventeen long Highland miles to the west—including a rare public trespass when the road jauntily abuts the frontage of the laird's Victorian mansion, Amhuinnsuidhe Castle—the determined traveller will arrive at Hushinish, where the hills sweep down to an incomparable bay. By some mysterious alchemy of sea and fall of hill, the truly golden scimitar of sand at Hushinish Bay has acquired the magical ambience of a great work of art.

Hushinish is the crossing point to the island of Scarp, scene of the most bizarre experiment ever undertaken by the Post Office. One Herr Zucker—a rocket inventor who must have had a beguiling line of sales patter—convinced the authorities in the unadventurous thirties that it was feasible to transport mail by rocket. A special stamp—'WESTERN ISLES ROCKET POST'—was produced, graphically illustrating the mail rocket in flaming flight. On 28 July 1936, Herr Zucker's theories were put to the test. His rocket lifted off from Scarp bound for the Harris shore. It exploded on impact, and the venture was abandoned. But the delighted philatelists whose mail was salvaged were left with unique first day covers of the one and only Western Isles Rocket Post.

North Uist, Benbecula and South Uist are linked by causeways and bridges across the treacherous tidal sands of the old North and South Ford. The shattered eastern seaboard from the Sound of Berneray to the South Ford merges imperceptibly into a spreading labyrinthe of fresh-water lochs. Summer brings an almost incandescent quality of light so that the glowing browns of the moor and peat bogs seem to intensify the brilliant blues of the lochans.

South Uist is the complete antithesis of the urban antheap; tiny crofting townships dotted with white-walled thatched cottages; black cattle grazing placidly on the fertile, flower-decked machair lands of the west coast; a life-style seemingly immune to the malaise of the money-bug. This is where the military have established a rocket range, but unlike Herr Zucker's they carry no mail and land in the Atlantic.

Barra is the smallest of the Western Isles; the perfect miniature. Flying to Barra aboard a light aircraft on a sunny day in May is as exhilarating an experience as life has to offer.

In by Barra Head over the great cliffs of Bernera, topped by the Barra Head Light 683-feet above high water. On over Barra's consorts—Mingulay, Pabbay, Sandray, Vatersay—and rock-like Kisimul Castle guarding the sea-ways to Castlebay. Dipping down over a jade green sea broken by the glittering expanse of the Traigh Mhor; Ben Eoligarry clothed with primroses; Atlantic rollers creaming on the white strand of the Traigh Uais; the sparkling cockle strand of the Traigh Mhor rushing up to meet the aircraft as it touches down on the silver shore.

38 A mere century ago Sutherland virtually belonged to one man. The Duke of Sutherland could claim title to 1,176,343 acres, ranging from the verdant shores of the Dornoch Firth to the remote wilderness of Cape Wrath. The ducal domain spanned the Highlands from east to west at its most scenifically magnificent, embracing a glittering host of rivers and lochs famed for their salmon and trout, glens and straths of a haunting beauty, and mountains of a singular grandeur.

The House of Sutherland reached the peak of its power in the late nineteenth century when the ducal name had become synonomous with the grim clearances that left the heart of Sutherland bereft of people and populated by sheep. The face of Sutherland was indelibly marked by that orgy of ruthless social engineering. Grass-grown ruins of crofting townships can be seen in many a deserted glen, mute testimony to the extent of the evictions. The legacy has been lasting; even today sheep outnumber human beings by more than twenty to one.

The natural gateway to Sutherland is Bonar Bridge, perched on the picturesque Kyle, where roads radiate to the east, north and west. The Kyle of Sutherland was first bridged — inevitably — by Thomas Telford in 1812. Telford's bridge was destroyed in the great flood of 1892, and its replacement, curiously enough, was destined for exactly the same life-span of 80 years. The present bridge, which was opened in 1973, retains much of the flavour of the original Telford design, and deservedly won the Structural Steel Design Award in 1974.

Golfers, caravaners, campers, and those with small children clamant for freedom from the confines of the family car, will be wise to branch east by the tree-flanked road along the shores of the Dornoch Firth. The road passes through the lush little hamlet of Spinningdale, with the cathedral-like ruins of its old cotton mill, and meanders on by Clashmore — notable for its imposing village hall clock tower — to Dornoch.

Dornoch has a dignity, spaciousness and style in keeping with its history as an ancient cathedral city. Sacked during the Reformation, the cathedral was reconstructed as a parish church in 1835 by the Sutherland family. It houses the marble tomb of the Marquess of Stafford, first Duke of Sutherland, who died in 1833 — according to the inscription — 'amidst the universal grief of his Scottish and English tenantry'.

A few minutes walk from the cathedral, and the golfing visitor is treading the sacred turf of the Royal Dornoch Golf Club, where the game was first played in 1616. It is a classic links course, flanked by little bays, where even the most fanatical aficionado must find his eyes straying to the wide expanse of beach as the long, low rollers sweep in on the immaculate sands.

The nearby caravan and camping site on the links accords to international standards. Mile upon mile of gently shelving sands ensure safe bathing, and unlimited scope for the pent up energies of the young.

The ducal village of Golspie is the seat of the Dukes of Sutherland's grandiose turreted palace, Dunrobin Castle. Dunrobin's formal gardens are laid out in the manner of Versailles — by no means a presumption given the regal dimensions of the castle—and the family museum affords fascinating insights into the life-style of the Sutherland grandees. Predictably stacked with trophies of the hunt from the farthest reaches of Empire, the museum also houses such singular memorabilia as the telephone from Dunrobin Private Railway Station, and a case

Sutherland

containing the 'Full Dress and Active Service Uniform and Accoutrements of the late Major the Lord Alistair St. C. Leveson-Gower, M.C.'

Wholly in keeping with the aura of Golspie is its superb miniature railway station, a gem of Victorian architecture. The inevitable marble plaque is to be found on the road bridge over the railway: *'This stone is placed here by the united subscription of all who were employed on the works of the Duke of Sutherland's Railway to record their sense of his patriotic munificence and zeal in promoting the industry and progress of the North of Scotland and in testimony of their respectful affection.'*

But the most extraordinary sight Golspie can offer is to be seen on top of the improbably named Ben Bhraggie. Stuck on the summit of the hill, mounted on a huge double plinth, is a giant statue of George Granville, the first Duke of Sutherland. Carved by Sir Francis Chantrey, the larger than life stone-faced duke gazes down upon the scenes of his former glory.

Unlike Golspie, Brora is an industrial village — quite the most attractive in Scotland — with a woollen mill, distillery and brickworks. Although coal seams were worked at Brora as far back as the sixteenth century, the village blossomed with the coming of the railway in 1870, and it has retained its splendidly Victorian character.

At the fishing village of Helmsdale further north, the railway line to Wick and Thurso plunges inland, following the course of the Helmsdale river up Strath Ullie. It was at Strath Ullie—the last glen to be cleared during the evictions—that the Great Sutherland Gold Rush took place in 1868. In a single year, the Highland prospectors washed nuggets and flakes of gold to the value of £12,000. Alarmed by such an invasion, the duke withdrew mining licenses, and had the diggers cleared from his land.

Another road from Bonar Bridge winds west along the Kyle of Sutherland under the wooded slopes of Balblair to Invershin. The north branch thrusts by the salmon-rich Shin to Lairg, scene every August of the biggest one-day lamb sale in Scotland.

North of Lairg the road crosses the empty wastes of the high moors—under the brooding peaks of Ben Loyal and Ben Hope—to the majestic sweep of the Kyle of Tongue, skirts the shores of lonely Loch Eriboll—which sheltered the war galleys of Haco seven centuries ago—and winds through Durness of the famous Smoo Caves.

Durness is the northernmost apex of the road; the point where it wheels south to explore the incomparable west. Once across the Kylesku ferry, take the winding road west through Drumbeg, past tiny lochans resplendent with water-lilies, opening on to vistas of Eddrachillis Bay, studded with innumerable green and rocky islets, to Stoer—and the exhilarating sweep down to Lochinver under the rearing primeval hump of Suilven.

It *is* incomparable.

It is the ultimate paradox to discover that the most northerly corner of the Scottish mainland is the least 'Highland' in character. Caithness is a snub-nosed triangular plateau of moors, inland lochs and extensive farmlands, bounded by the North Sea, the Pentland Firth and the Atlantic Ocean. Those tumultuous seas have shaped a fortress coastline of formidable cliffs. Detached stacks — besieged outposts resisting the assaults of the enemy to the end — rise above the waves like stranded keeps.

Away from the sea and the cliffs, the gently rolling farmlands are thick with cattle. It is the definitive Caithness landscape — well-husbanded, trim and ordered — but with unique features. Flagstoned dykes mark the boundaries of fields, and provide highly practical windbreaks. Tower silos point high above farm steadings as far as the eye can see, and the uncongested roads allow such ease of movement that the overall effect is one of untrammelled space under the big Caithness sky.

It was 1811 before the first road ventured over the border from Sutherland into Caithness. Before that momentous day even the hardiest traveller dreaded crossing the granite promontory of the wild Ord of Caithness. Nowadays, it is an exhilarating drive. Across the Ord, the road plummets down into Berriedale, nestling in the hollow of its wooded strath.

Lybster has pretensions above its station. The main street of the village is a positive boulevard, with a bank in proportion, grandiose enough to gratify the touchiest oil sheik. But Lybster's gem is its harbour.

Scalloped out of a green hill, it is the work of Telford's protege, the great Joseph Mitchell. "I am convinced," observed Mitchell, "that instead of running our artificial piers into the sea, involving such serious risk of destruction, harbours even of refuge might be constructed with more safety and greater economy, by excavating *inwards*."

After erecting a pier-head at the entrance, that is exactly what he did, creating space for the small coastal vessels of the nineteenth century, and several hundred fishing boats. With its old mill on the river bank, Joseph Mitchell's Lybster Harbour is a picture-postcard haven of green.

Sir John Sinclair of Ulbster, Parliamentarian, agricultural innovator and writer extraordinary — 367 works are attributed to him — created the invaluable 'Statistical Account of Scotland'. It first appeared in 1791, and informed the wider world — in the great understatement of all time — of the wondrous Whaligoe Steps.

"The fishermen on this part of the coast, to get to their boats descend a huge precipice by winding steps in the face of the rock, by which some lives have been lost; and yet, from frequent practice, it is often done without assistance by a blind fisherman in Ulbster. To secure their boats from being dashed against the rocks, particularly in storms, the fishermen hang up their yawls by ropes on hooks fixed in the face of the rock, where they are safely suspended till the weather is fit for going to sea. Mr. Brodie, tacksman of Ulbster, has paid some attention to rendering the passage easier down the declivity."

Whatever the attentions of Mr. Brodie, the spectacle of this stupendous stairway winding down the face of the cliff to the cove at the bottom concentrates the mind on the heroic labours of those who achieved the seemingly impossible.

Caithness

The huge Caithness flags forming the steps — and those buttressing the turns — have become almost a part of the cliff, grass-grown and flower-decked in summer. The store shed on the little quay — its seaward wall seeming a part of the rock from which it rises — stands open to the sky, and an old derrick lies athwart the quay beside the skeletal black timbers of a long-dead boat. But the ring bolts are still intact, firmly anchored in the rock face where the yawls once hung.

When green rollers break on Whaligoe, and the black head of a seal bobs in the spume among the rocks at the mouth of the cove, the ghosts of the fishermen of old gather. Easy to see them setting out in their frail craft to brave the perilous northern seas for the silver herring. And who can climb the 338 steps that remain without thinking of those men and women who footed it up the cliff in all weathers, burdened with creels of fish on their backs? The Whaligoe Steps are the testimony in stone of a people driven to superhuman exertions in the harsh struggle for survival.

Robert Louis Stevenson spent part of his boyhood in Wick when his father was supervising the construction of the great breakwater. A plaque above the door of the Stevensons' lodgings in Harbour Street — now the Customs Office — records the author's stay. In those days, Wick was the frenetic centre of the booming herring industry; the harbour a dense forest of masts. Nostalgia haunts the quiet harbour today, and the old grey town has a languid air.

But Wick has the first new glass factory to be built in Scotland this century, and thousands of visitors come to see the youthful glass-blowers — all local boys — working at their ancient craft.

At John O'Groats you really do have the feeling of standing on land's end, with John O'Groats House Hotel serving as a beacon.

Thurso underwent a population explosion with the advent of the Atomic Energy Authority's Dounreay project, but the old and the new have coalesced with surprising ease. It is a town with architectural style.

The science-fiction steel containment sphere of the veteran Dounreay Fast Reactor still has the power to startle when seen against the rocks and sea of the Caithness coast, although it is now dwarfed — in nuclear technology as well as size — by its gargantuan big brother, the Prototype Fast Reactor.

No traveller should fail to pause at Reay, and climb the quaint flagstone steps over the wall into the old burial ground. It is a good place to salute the memory of the Rev. Alexander Pope, one time parish minister of Reay. A man of exceptional strength, the Rev. Pope selected his elders on the grounds of their physique. Sinners were often forcibly overpowered and carted off to the kirk by the reverend and his strong-arm squad of elders. Dedicated to his own peculiar brand of muscular Christianity, Mr. Pope always carried a thick cudgel, and he was not averse to thumping wayward parishioners.

In the summer of 1732 this extraordinary clergyman mounted his pony and rode all the way to Twickenham to pay his respects to his namesake, Alexander Pope the poet. Even after that daunting literary pilgrimage, he had the strength to make the return journey.

West from Reay the road wanders over the moorland to Kyle of Tongue and the beckoning mountains of Sutherland; a route loved by the muscular Alexander Pope.

42 Orkney is the richest archaeological treasure trove in all Britain. The western arm of the Loch of Harray noses towards the Bay of Skaill on the Atlantic shore of the West Mainland; the southern arm of the loch divides the burial cairn of Maeshowe from the megalithic Standing Stones of Stenness and the Ring of Brodgar.

All that can be seen of Maeshowe from the outside is a great circular mound rising to a height of 24 feet. The entrance is by means of a low, shoulder-width passage 36 feet in length. Rectangular recesses lead off from three sides of the square main chamber. The openings to the three recesses are raised three feet above the level of the chamber floor.

Mere statistics are puny pointers; they cannot convey the heroic scale of such a colossal labour of construction in the dawn of history by a people with only the crudest of implements. But there is nothing crude about the masonry of Maeshowe. The stones are set with such mathematical precision that the unknown master builder could have had little to learn about the science of geometry.

Four thousand years ago these unknown men of Orkney bore the remains of their great ones to Maeshowe and buried them within the three innermost chambers, sealing the tomb with a huge block of stone. The unknown people left no written records. All that is marked on the ancient stones of this awesome fortress of the dead is the runic graffiti scratched by a band of marauding Norsemen who broke into the burial chamber in search of treasure. And Maeshowe had housed its mysterious dead for three thousand years before the Norse pillagers penetrated the tomb.

Age-old mysteries abound. On the narrow spit of land between the Lochs of Harray and Stenness the gaunt megaliths of the Ring of Brodgar and the Standing Stones of Stenness cast their brooding aura over moor and water. But a little further west the intimate domestic life-style of the first Orcadians has been miraculously revealed.

In the winter of 1850 a great storm, sweeping in from the Atlantic, shifted the high dune of Skara Brae in the south corner of the Bay of Skaill and exposed the stonework of prehistoric buidlings, Skilled excavations, over a period of eighty years, have uncovered a cluster of stone-built dwellings connected by a maze of passages, covered alleyways and a paved open court, forming a complex, enclosed communal settlement. The single-room dwellings with their central fireplaces, box beds, stone dressers and wall cupboards present a vivid picture of the manner in which this tiny pastoral community dwelt on the edge of the great ocean at Skara Brae.

But there is much more to the Orkney story than the astonishing artefacts of the first Orcadians. Warriors, poets and mystics have played a tempestuous—often murderous—part in shaping the destiny of these islands; a curious quirk of history when the slow-paced, measured equilibrium of life in the Orkney Isles is one of its greatest attractions today.

In Holy Week 1116, the cousins Hakon Paulson and Magnus Erlendson, joint inheritors of the Norse Jarldom of Orkney, met on the tranquil little island of Egilsay to settle the bloody factional strife between their followers. The unwordly Magnus presented himself as a sacrifice, and was slain by Hakon's cook Lifolf; a deed that ensured the

Orkney

cook's name an infamous immortality in the Sagas.

Rognvald Kolson—poet, warrior, statesman, pilgrim to Jerusalem, and nephew of the martyred Magnus—vowed to build a stone minster *'more magnificent than any other in these lands'* in memory of his saintly uncle. The first blocks of sandstone were laid in the year 1137, and the patient work of centuries was begun.

The cathedral church of St. Magnus the Martyr is the pride and glory of Kirkwall. Rising in splendour from the historic heart of the town, it is a noble fulfilment of an ancient vow. But the cathedral is only part of an architectural heritage that never fails to astound the newcomer. Even the ruins of the Earl's Palace nearby retain such a sumptuous Renaissance panache that one could readily imagine Cesare Borgia, accompanied by a retinue of haughty Florentine nobles, emerging from within its walls.

Kirkwall stands on the isthmus where the East and West Mainland meet; the natural fulcrum of the corporate life of the scattered flotilla of North Isles. Kirkwall's airport at Grimsetter stables a sturdy little work-horse of an aircraft, appropriately named the *Islander*. This inter-island air-bus has revolutionised transport. The first lighthouse in Orkney, at Dennis Head, North Ronaldsay, came into service in 1789, the year of the French Revolution. In those days, service on the Dennis Head Light must have seemed like exile to the edge of the world. Nowadays, the keeper of the new Light on North Ronaldsay can wait until he sees the *Islander* approaching before leaving for the landing strip and a swift flight to Kirkwall.

On the West Mainland the little town of Stromness—known to the Norsemen as Hamnavoe, the haven inside the bay—clings to the crescent shore of its landlocked harbour under the lee of Brinkie's Brae. From five houses on the foreshore in 1642, Stromness grew throughout the eighteenth century, gradually toiling up the steep hillside wherever the lie of the land provided a site.

The narrow, flagstoned main street — *'uncoiled like a sailer's rope,'* as Orkney's greatest writer, George Mackay Brown, describes it—makes a whimsical progression. Shop windows reach down almost to ground level; gable ends meet like castle keeps above pencil-thin lanes sloping down to the harbour. Stromness was a thriving seaport in the days of sail, and the salt tang of its history lingers on.

The South Isles of Hoy—Haey, 'the high island' of the Norsemen—Burray and South Ronaldsay form the enclosing arms of Scapa Flow, the major naval base of the Home Fleet in two world wars. On the night of 14 October 1939 the battleship *Royal Oak* lay at anchor in the Flow, and was torpedoed by a German U-boat. The sinking of the *Royal Oak* brought about the building of causeways—the Churchill Barriers—between the islands of Lambs Holm, Glimps Holm, Burray and South Ronaldsay, all of which are now linked by road to the village of St. Mary's on Mainland Orkney.

The giant dreadnoughts, bristling with armaments, which once lorded the waters of Scapa Flow are no more than a memory. Giant skate and halibut are now the centre of attention, as the sheltered waters of the Flow increasingly attract sea anglers. It is a fitting metamorphosis; one wholly in keeping with the history and tradition of Orkney.

44 When the Romans first sighted the Shetland archipelago they named it—in the high Roman fashion—*Ultima Thule*. And it was a Roman historian, Caius Cornelius Tacitus, who penned the classic description of these singular islands. His words have endured for almost 2,000 years, for the very good reason that they have never been bettered.

'Nowhere,' wrote Tacitus, 'does the sea hold wider sway; it carries to and fro in its actions a mass of currents, and in its ebb and flow it is not held by the coast but penetrates deep into the land and winds about in the hills, as if in its own domain.'

Shetland's unique quality lies not merely in the physical characteristics of the islands, singular though they undoubtedly are, but in the atmosphere that permeates them. Not Highland, not Scottish, not British, the people of Shetland have clung tenaciously to a cohesive island identity that is distinctively Norse.

Half a millennium has passed since the penurious King Christian of Denmark, unable to raise the agreed marriage dowry on the wedding of his daughter to James III of Scotland, chucked in Shetland as part payment. It was a bad deal for the Shetlanders. The ruthless oppression they endured at the hands of the rapacious Scottish feudal barons is the reason why they have never lost an awareness of their own non-Scottish history. Even today, 'The Mainland' for them is their own principal island—Mainland. Leaving for the Scottish mainland, they talk unselfconsciously of "going to Scotland."

Fair Isle is the southernmost outpost; a lonestepping stone in the waste of sea between Orkney and Shetland. The island is one of the world's most remarkable staging posts for migratory birds. In the last thirty years around 300 species have been recorded, and more than 81,000 birds have been trapped, examined and ringed.

Apart from its galaxy of migrants, Fair Isle has vast colonies of breeding seabirds. The clownish Puffins abound in thousands around the island's coast; Fulmars, once rare, now crowd teeming tenements on the cliffs, and Razorbills, Guillemots, Kittiwakes, Bonzies and Artic Skuas all thrive—an arrogant colony of Skuas having selected the fringes of the island's airstrip as their breeding ground.

The new bird observatory and hostel has attracted visitors from all over the world. Cedar-built and superbly situated looking out on the majestic Sheep Rock—a green-topped, horseshoe-shaped throne fit for a giant from Norse mythology—the observatory provides an ideal haven for bird watchers or those who simply want to relish an environment free of the slightest taint of commercial exploitation.

Sumburgh airport, at the toe of the long leg of Mainland, hotches with helicopters, whirling the helmeted oilmen to their man-made islands of steel in the distant Shetland waters. Every time they lift off from Sumburgh, they have a bird's-eye view of Jarlshof, where painstaking excavation has uncovered village settlements spanning 4,000 years of human occupation. There is something infinitely moving in the sight of the domestic arrangements of the Neolithic settlers of Jarlshof who lived by the sea so long ago.

It is always the sea that is at the heart of the Shetland scene; all-pervasive, the constant catalyst that has shaped the lives of countless generations of Shetlanders. Whether creaming over the black teeth of distant skerries, or flailing the rockface of Eshaness and roaring inland

Shetland

into the Holes of Scraada, or gently washing the sheltered green shores of tranquil voes, or lapping Lerwick's crowded waterfront, the sea is the insistent interloper, never out of sight or sound.

'We anchored in Bressay Sound in front of the town of Lerwick,' wrote the young Joseph Mitchell in 1829 on his first visit to Shetland as the newly appointed engineer for the northern harbours. *'Here was a curious and interesting scene, the town emerging, as it were, out of the sea. In the bay, which was narrow and landlocked, besides a few small British vessels, there were anchored about 120 Dutch fishing busses, and a number of wherries moving to and fro. Dutchmen have fished in these waters from time immemorial. The vessels are large and well formed, having one large lug sail, and they float like ducks on the water. Of course a good deal of smuggling occurs between them and the inhabitants'.*

The Dutch busses which once crowded Lerwick harbour are a mere folk memory. But still to be seen are the tall houses rising out of the sea rubbing conspiratorial shoulders with enclosed wharves and shuttered warehouses that once harboured cargoes of contraband in the days when smuggling was an integral part of the Shetland way of life.

'Lanes and stairs lead up from the sea,' young Mitchell observed, *'to the principal street, which is very narrow and paved with flags.'*

Happily, Lerwick's beguiling 'principal street'—Commercial Street—is still paved with flags, and mysterious, arrow-thin lanes and stairs still thrust down to the waterfront. Fishermen from every seafaring nation in Europe know them well; the American oilmen are simply the latest in a long line of migrants to have sought refuge from the wild northern seas in this the least parochial small town in Scotland.

The fishing port of Scalloway was the old capital of Shetland. Earl Patrick's ruined castle, with its flamboyant corbelled turrets, overlooks the harbour. The green and fertile valley of the Loch of Tingwall ranges inland where the *Althing*—the ancient Parliament of the islands—was reputedly located.

Out Skerries is the tiny eastern outrider of the close-clustered North Isles—Whalsay, Fetlar, Yell and Unst. By a miraculous accident of nature, the islands of Grunay, Bruray and Housay form a ring of shields creating a sheltered lagoon in the wilds of the North Sea. That lagoon-like harbour is the fulcrum of life in Out Skerries, where a tiny community leads its own good life and wrests a living from the sea.

In 1967 a pair of Snowy Owls nested on a hill in Fetlar. It was one of the great ornithological events of the century. 1400 acres surrounding the hill has been designated a Statutory Bird Reserve, to the evident satisfaction of the new settlers.

Shetland ponies are reared in freedom on the high scattald—the common grazings—of Unst, the most northerly isle of all. The great cliffs of Hermaness swarm with immense flocks of nesting seabirds—Gannets, Guillemots, Razorbills, Puffins and Shags—whose incessant, argumentative clamour overlays the crashing of the Atlantic breakers.

A mile offshore from Hermaness—best seen from Saxavord – the Muckle Flugga Lighthouse confronts the seas from its lonely rock. Beyond Muckle Flugga there is only an immensity of ocean, bounded by the Artic Circle. It is a sight to cut man's pretensions down to size.

explore

Maps and gazetteers

Listed and numbered

Buildings & Castles	Information Centres
Monuments & Sites	Chairlifts
Geographical features	Forests (named)
Museums	Forest Parks (named)
Other places of interest	Nature Reserves (numbered)
Gardens	N.T. Outlines (numbered)
Bird Sanctuaries	

The following, although NOT listed in the gazetteers, are shown on the maps:

Camp & Caravan Sites	Seal sightings
Golf courses	Sub aqua
Fishing Harbours	GARVE Railways & Stas.
Day cruise centres	Airports
Lighthouses	Airstrips
Pony trekking	Car Ferries
Sea angling	Canals
Sailing schools	Hydro-electric dams
Youth hostels	Beaches

Example

In the Oban, Mull and District gazetteer:
To find Ardchattan Priory look on the map for the 'Buildings and Castles' symbol — 🏰 — with **1** beside it.

🏰   BUILDINGS AND CASTLES

1   **Ardchattan Priory**
Remains of 13th C monastery of the Valliscaulian order destroyed by Cromwell's troops in 1654. Mostly ruinous but incorporating a private house (occasionally open to public). (See also GARDENS). (AM).

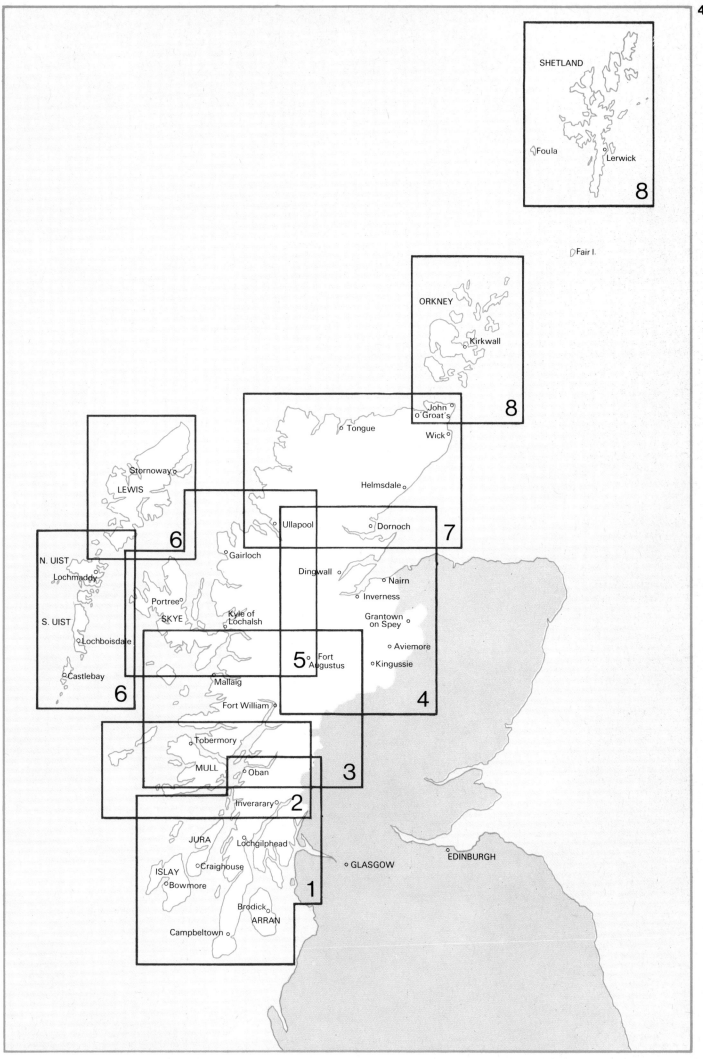

SHETLAND

Foula

Lerwick

8

Fair I.

ORKNEY

Kirkwall

7

8

John
o'Groat's

Tongue

Wick

Stornoway

LEWIS

6

Helmsdale

Ullapool

Dornoch

7

N. UIST

Lochmaddy

Gairloch

Dingwall

Nairn

Inverness

S. UIST

Portree

SKYE

Kyle of
Lochalsh

Grantown
on Spey

Aviemore

Lochboisdale

6

Mallaig

5

Fort
Augustus

Kingussie

4

Castlebay

6

Fort William

Tobermory

MULL

Oban

3

Inverarary

2

JURA

Lochgilphead

ISLAY

Craighouse

GLASGOW

EDINBURGH

Bowmore

1

Brodick

ARRAN

Campbeltown

BUILDINGS AND CASTLES

Arran

1   Brodick Castle
This ancient seat of the Dukes of Hamilton dating from the 14th century, includes a considerable part of the Beckford collection, and silver, porcelain, sporting pictures and trophies. Open: Easter, then May to September. Open on certain other dates in April. Tel: 0770 2202. Admission charges on application (NTS) (see also GARDENS).

2   High Corrie
Good example of a Scottish *clachan* comprising eight dwellings.

3   Kildonan Castle
A ruined tower-house.

4   Lochranza Castle
Substantial remains of what is probably a 16th century building. The existence of a castle on this site was first recorded at the end of the 14th C (AM).

Dunoon, Cowal and Bute

5   Carrick Castle, Lochgoil
Ruined 14th C castle.

6   Castle Lachlan, Strathlachlan
13th C castle overlooking Loch Fyne, now a ruin. No entry fee.

7   Kames Castle
14th C tower and castle. Tower is now a children's home. Not open to the public.

8   Kilmun Collegiate Church
Founded in 1442 by an ancestor of the Argylls and burial place of ducal family.

9   Old Mansion House, Rothesay
Built in 1681 the house is a good example of Scottish architecture of this period.

9   Rothesay Castle
Partially ruined mediaeval castle dating from early 13th C. The walls, heightened and provided with four round towers in the late 13th C, enclose a circular courtyard, unique in Scotland. Entry fee charged.

9   St. Mary's Chapel, Rothesay
Late mediaeval remains of the Abbey Church of St. Mary. Entry fee charged.

Mid Argyll, Kintyre and Islay

10   Carnasserie Castle, Kilmartin
Remains of 16th C fortified castle built by John Carswell, first Protestant Bishop of the Isles, who translated Knox's Liturgy into Gaelic. (AM).

11   Castle Sween
12th C ruin, on south shore of Loch Sween. (AM).

12   Circular Church, Bowmore
Dating from 1769, the church is reputedly built in this shape to prevent the devil hiding in corners. Visitors welcome.

13   Inverarary Castle
18th C building containing fine tapestries, portraits, furniture and china. Home of Dukes of Argyll since 15th C. Enquire locally about admission.

13   Old Town House, Inveraray
Built in 18th C and now used as municipal building. Houses Tourist Information Centre.

14   Oronsay Priory
Remains of 14th C priory.

15   Saddell Abbey, Kintyre
Founded in 12th C. Contains some fine tombstones. No entry fee charged.

16   Tarbert Castle
Remains of 15th C keep on site of earlier castles. No entry fee charged.

♏ MONUMENTS AND SITES

Arran

1   Auchagallon Stone Circle
A Bronze Age burial cairn surrounded by a circle of fifteen standing stones (AM).

2   Carn Ban
One of the most famous of the Neolithic long cairns in SW Scotland. (AM).

3   Memorial Seat
On the Brodick / Lamlash road, an unusual memorial with designs derived from the island's prehistoric monuments.

4   Moss Farm Road Stone Circle
Machrie Moor Bronze Age Stone Circles and Neolithic chambered tombs. There are six stone circles, close to the old cart track passing the Moss Farm, and two Neolithic tombs. Some of the stones are as much as 16 ft. high and the area, comprising about a mile of moorland, is of outstanding archaeological interest and includes Moss Farm Road Stone Circle and Standing Stones of Tormore. (AM).

5   Torr a'Chaisteal
Circular Iron Age fort now largely buried. (AM).

6   Torrylin Cairn
A Neolithic chambered cairn of which four segments of the chamber survive. (AM).

Dunoon, Cowal and Bute

7   Dunagoil Vitrified Fort, Bute
Iron Age vitrified fort excavated in the early 20th C, which contained a wealth of relics giving information about the inhabitants. No entry fee.

8   Dunbirgidale, Bute
Iron Age fort with wall chamber and buttress walls. No entry fee.

9   Glecknabae Cairn, Bute
Neolithic cairn with ruined chamber and cists. No entry fee.

10   Glenvoidean Cairn, Bute
Neolithic cairn with three chambers, forecourt and side walls visible. No entry fee.

11   Higland Mary Statue, Dunoon
Unveiled in 1896 to commemorate Mary Campbell — Robert Burns' "Highland Mary". No entry fee.

12   Kilfinan Churchyard
On site of early church dedicated to Finan — a monk from Iona. No entry fee.

11   Lamont Memorial, Dunoon
Granite memorial to the 36 members of the Lamont family hanged in 1646 by troops of the Marquis of Argyll. No entry fee.

Mid Argyll, Kintyre and Islay

13   Davaar Island
Cave painting by unknown artist.

14   Dunadd Hill, Lochgilphead
Hill fort dating from Dark Ages. Identified as the capital and crowning place of early kings of Dalriada. (AM).

15   Kilmartin Carved Cross
An ancient carved cross inside a War Memorial Gateway.

15   Kilmartin Churchyard
In the churchyard is a cross dating from about 16th C and mediaeval sculptured stones. (AM).

16   Kilmichael Glassary
Cup-and-ring engravings dating from about 2000-1500 BC on natural rock outcrop. (AM). No entry fee charged.

17   Poltalloch Monuments, Kilmartin
Standing stone and gravestones of Malcolm chiefs. (AM). No entry fee charged.

18   St. Columba's Footprints, Keil
Footprints cut into a rock believed to mark spot where St. Columba first landed.

19   Sculptured Celtic Crosses, Kildalton and Kilchoman
Dating from about 15th C Kildaltan is one of the finest Celtic crosses still in existence. Kilchoman Cross dates from about same time and stands 8 ft. high

★ GEOGRAPHICAL FEATURES

Arran

1   Columnar Cliffs, Drumadoon
Approached either along the shore from Blackwaterfoot, or via the golf course, the high cliff is most spectacular, resembling the rocks at Fingal's Cave.

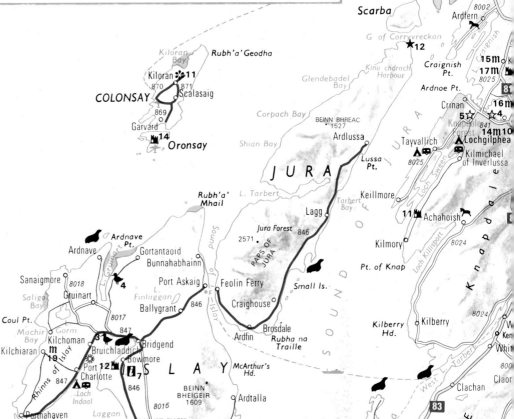

0   10 Miles

© MAP PRODUCTIONS LTD.

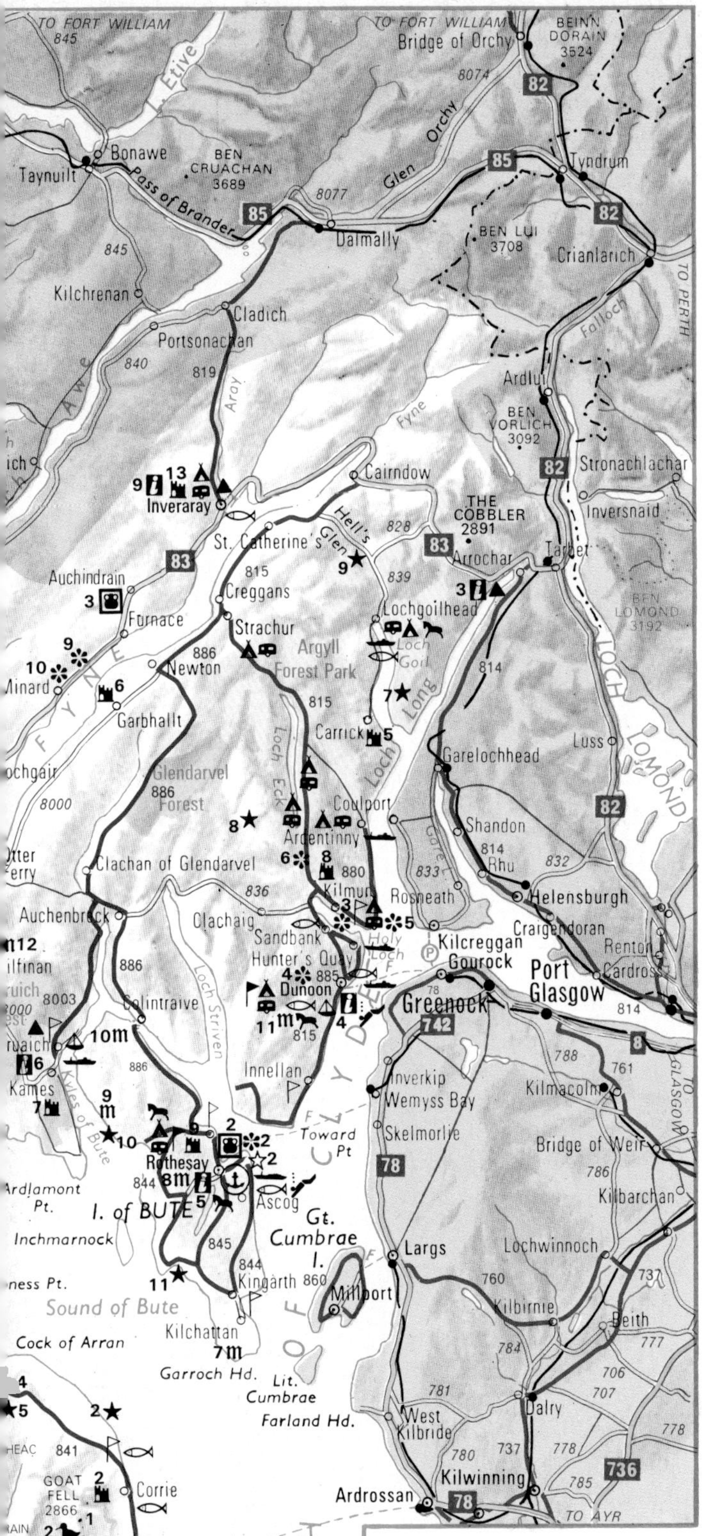

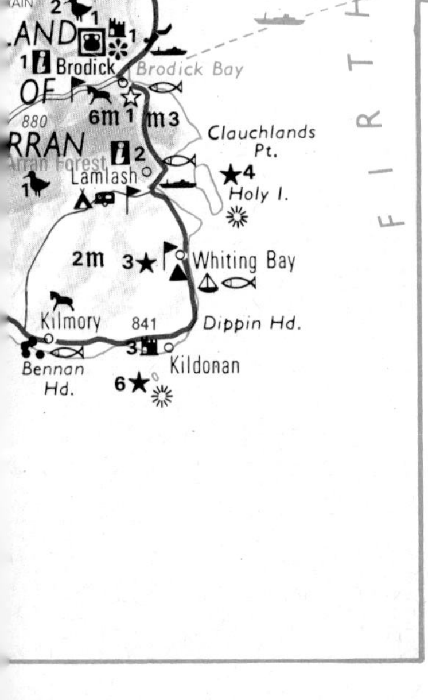

2 **Fallen Rocks, North Sannox**
Reached via the picnic area at North Sannox and the Forestry road along the shore.

3 **Glen Ashdale**
A wooded glen with a spectacular 200 ft. waterfall. Nature trail.

4 **Holy Isle**
Island off Lamlash with central peak rising to over 1,000 ft. On the island is St. Molais's Cave, the cell of a hermit in the days of St. Columba. Visit by ferry from Lamlash.

5 **Lochranza**
The 'Fairy Dell' and geological features 'The Rents' at Scriodan and Hutton's Unconformity.

6 **Pladda**
Island off the south east coast.

Dunoon, Cowal and Bute

7 **Argyll's Bowling Green**
Range of hills over 2000 ft. high.

8 **Falls of Massan**
Most picturesque glen in Cowal.

9 **Hell's Glen**
Forbidding pass in the hills between Loch Fyne and Loch Goil.

10 **Kyles of Bute**
Narrow stretches of water separating Bute from Argyll mainland. Cruises available.

11 **Scalpsie, Bute**
Beach of red sand.

Mid Argyll, Kintyre and Islay

12 **Corryvrechan Whirlpool**
Dangerous whirlpool between islands of Jura and Scarba. View from North Jura.

MUSEUMS

Arran

1 **Arran Museum — Old Smiddy, Rosaburn, Brodick**
Museum in process of being established.

Dunoon, Cowal and Bute

2 **Bute Natural History Museum, Rothesay**
Entry fee charged.

Mid Argyll, Kintyre and Islay

3 **Auchindrain Museum of Farming Life**
Entry Fee charged. Open April-October; Mon-Sat. 10 a.m. to 6 p.m.; Sun. 2 p.m. to 6 p.m.

4 **Campbeltown Museum**
No entry fee charged. Open week days.

OTHER PLACES OF INTEREST

Arran

1 **Arran Nature Centre**
Exhibitions and information on natural history of Arran. Entry fee charged.

Dunoon, Cowal and Bute

2 **Bute Nature Trails**
Six walking trails and one motor trail devised by Bute Natural History Society. Full details locally.

2 **Library and Leisure Centre, Rothesay**

2 **Winter Garden, Rothesay**

Mid Argyll, Kintyre and Islay

3 **Carradale Information Centre**
Entry fee charged (FC) (See also FORESTS).

4 **Crinan Canal**
Designed by Sir John Rennie in 1793 and opened in 1801.

5 **Knapdale Forest Centre**
Entry fee charged (FC). (See also FORESTS).

GARDENS

Arran

1 **Brodick Castle Gardens**
Two gardens — the woodland garden was started in 1923 and is now one of the finest rhododendron gardens in Britain, if not in Europe. The formal garden dates from 1710.

Dunoon, Cowal and Bute

2 **Esplanade, Rothesay**
Tropical palm trees alongside rock gardens and exotic shrubs. No entry fee.

3 **Kilmun Arboretum**
150 acres offering a variety of ornamental shrubs and trees in Argyll Forest Park. Guide book available. (FC) (See also FOREST PARKS).

4 **Morag's Fairy Glen, Dunoon**
Miniature forest garden. No entry fee charged.

2 **Rothesay Nurseries, Ardencraig**
Entry Fee charged.

5 **Strone, Cairndow**
Daffodils and rhododendrons. Entry fee charged.

6 **Younger Botanic Gardens, Benmore**
Extensive woodland gardens featuring rhododendrons, azaleas and shrubs. Entry fee charged.

Mid Argyll, Kintyre and Islay

7 **Achamore Garden, Gigha**
Famed for spring flowers, roses and rare sub-tropical shrubs and plants. Donations.

8 **Carradale House, Kintyre**
Attractive garden on east coast of Mull of Kintyre. Donations from visitors. For opening hours inquire locally.

9 **Crarae Forest Garden**
Contains 107 plots of conifers and specimen trees. Admission during daylight hours. No entry fee. (FC).

10 **Crarae Lodge, Minard**
Woodland garden with collection of rhododendrons and exotic trees and shrubs. Donations from visitors. Open daily April 2 — September 30.

11 **Kiloran House, Colonsay**
Island garden noted for rhododendrons and shrubs. Donations from visitors. For opening times inquire locally.

BIRD SANCTUARIES AND OBSERVATION POINTS

Arran

1 **Bird Life**
Over 100 species of birds found on the island, notably birds of prey.

2 **Glen Rosa**
Golden Eagle, peregrine falcon, buzzard, sparrow hawk, hen harrier, etc. (NTS) (See also NATIONAL TRUST FOR SCOTLAND ESTATES).

Mid Argyll, Kintyre and Islay

3 **Head of Loch Indaal**
Waders and wildfowl, especially barnacle geese and scaup.

4 **Loch Gruinart**
Wildfowl and waders, especially barnacle geese.

5 **Mull of Kintyre**
Migration observation point.

6 **Mull of Oa, Islay**
Bird cliffs.

TOURIST INFORMATION CENTRES

Arran

1 **Brodick**
Situated at Brodick Pier. May to September — open 9 a.m. to 7.30 p.m. October to May — open during arrival and departure times of ferry. Tel: Brodick 2401 and 2140.

2 **Lamlash**
Council Offices, Lamlash. Open all year, Monday to Friday — 9 a.m. to 5 p.m. Tel: Lamlash 385.

Dunoon, Cowal and Bute

3 **Ardgartan** (S) Tel: Arrochar 388

4 **Dunoon**
Pier Esplanade. Tel: Dunoon 3785

5 **Rothesay** Main Pier Approach. Tel: 2151

6 **Tighnabruaich** (S) Tel: Tighnabruaich 393

Mid Argyll, Kintyre and Islay

7 **Bowmore** (S) Tel: 049 681 254

8 **Campbeltown** The Pier. Tel: 0586 2056.

9 **Inveraray** (S) Tel: 0499 2063

10 **Lochgilphead** (S) Tel: 0546 2344

11 **Tarbert** (S) Tel: 088 02 429

FOREST PARKS

Dunoon, Cowal and Bute

Argyll Forest Park
About 95 square miles of forest and mountain between Loch Long, Loch Goil and Loch Eck. Includes forests of Glenbranter, Benmore and Ardgartan. Forest walks, camp site, picnic area, Kilmun Arboretum. Main access is A83, (Tarbert-Inveraray). Guide book from forest office and camp sites. (FC) (See also GARDENS).

FORESTS

Arran

Arran Forest
Information from Forestry Commision Office, Brodick.

Dunoon, Cowal and Bute

Ardgartan Forest
(See under Argyll Forest Park) Caravan, camping site NN 275030 on A83, two miles south of Arrochar. April-October. Walking, climbing; fishing permits for River Goil from forest office. Picnic place — Glenmore NN 202062, B828.

Benmore Forest
(See under Argyll Forest Park) Forest walks — Black Gates and Puck's Glen on A815, 6-7 miles north of Dunoon. All year. Kilmun Arboretum — NS 165821 on A880 (Kilmun-Ardentinny): booklet.

Glenbranter Forest
(See under Argyll Forest Park) Walking routes — information at forest office. NS 110974 from A815, 3 miles south-east of Strachur. Picnic places on Loch Eck side

Glendarvel Forest
Caladh Castle Forest Trail: NS 001760 on A8003 (Glendarvel-Tighnabruaich) Booklet from forest office. All year. Car park and picnic places south of Kames on unclassified road to Ardlamont Point and at Portavadie.

Tighnabruaich Forest
Photo-safari hides for viewing wild ducks, roe deer and blue hares. Picnic area, forest trail, guide map. Entry fee for hides. (FC).

Mid Argyll, Kintyre and Islay

Carradale Forest
Information centre and four walks at NR 799382 on B879 from B842 (Skipness-Campbeltown). All year. (FC). Picnic area. (See also OTHER PLACES OF INTEREST).

Inverliever Forest
Forest trail and 9 walks from NM 969126 on unclassified but well surfaced road on west side of Loch Awe joining B845 from Taynuilt to B840 at Ford, beginning journey from A85 (Dalmally-Oban) or A816 (Lochgilphead-Oban). All year. Booklet from local shop and Forestry Commision office. 15 holiday houses, Dalavich. Three picnic areas. (FC).

Knapdale Forest
Information centre and 5 walks from NR 790910 from Lochgilphead-Oban road at Cairnbaan on B841 then B8025 at Ballanoch for one mile. Holiday house, Achnacara. Picnic area. (FC) (See also OTHER PLACES OF INTEREST).

NATIONAL NATURE RESERVES

Arran

Glen Diomham
Contains two species of Service Tree which in Britain occur only in North Arran. (NCC).

NATIONAL TRUST FOR SCOTLAND ESTATES

Arran

Goatfell and Glen Rosa
Goatfell is Arran's highest peak (2866 ft.) and commands impressive views. Glen Rosa is of considerable ornithological interest. (NTS) (See also BIRD SANCTUARIES AND OBSERVATION POINTS).

🏰 BUILDINGS AND CASTLES

1 Ardchattan Priory
Remains of 13th C monastery of the Valliscaulian order destroyed by Cromwell's troops in 1654. Mostly ruinous but incorporating a private house (occasionally open to public). (See also GARDENS). (AM).

2 Barcaldine Castle
Early 17th C tower-house restored at beginning of 20th C. Private house, sometimes open to public.

3 Castle Coeffin, Lismore
Ruined castle on attractive site on west coast of island. Visit by ferry from Oban, then 3 mile walk. No entry fee charged.

4 Castle Stalker, Appin
16th C tower-house on small island now being restored by private owner. Not open to public.

5 Duart Castle, Mull
Built in 13th C, ruined and restored this century to present appearance. Open May-Sept, Mon-Fri, 10.30 am to 6 pm and July-Aug, Sunday 2.30 pm to 6 pm. Entry fee charged.

6 Dunollie Castle
Ruined 15th C tower-house and bailey on cliff site, north end of Oban Bay: fortified for some 1200 years. Not open to public.

7 Dunstaffnage Castle
13th C with later additions. In good state of preservation. Stone of Destiny said to have been kept on this site before its removal to Scone. (AM). Open standard hours.

8 Gylen Castle, Kerrera
Small, ruined tower-house (1587, sacked 1647) in superb setting at south end of island. No entry fee charged.

9 Iona Abbey
Founded in 6th C by St Columba; site restored and maintained by Iona Community. Present buildings date from 13th C onwards. No entry fee charged.

10 Kilchurn Castle
Ruined castle, built in 1440, and extended by Sir John Campbell (1635-1716). No entry fee charged. (AM).

11 St Moluag's Cathedral, Lismore
Dating from 13th C; the choir, much restored, is still in use as a church.

12 St Oran's Cemetery (Reilig Odhrain), Iona
Burial ground of 48 Scottish kings. No entry fee charged.

♏ MONUMENTS AND SITES

1 Duncan Ban Macintyre Monument, Dalmally
Monument to a bard who has been described as the 'Burns of the Highlands'.

2 McCaig's Tower, Oban
Similar in style to the Colosseum, the tower was built in 1890 by McCaig to provide work for the unemployed. Interior laid out as garden. No entry fee charged.

3 MacQuarrie Tomb, Gruline
Monument to Major-General MacQuarrie, first Governor-General of New South Wales, who founded the village of Salen in 1808.

4 Nelson Monument, Taynuilt
Standing stone re-erected as monument to Lord Nelson by English immigrants who worked in the local iron-smelter which closed in 1874.

★ GEOGRAPHICAL FEATURES

1 Fingal's Cave, Staffa
Spectacular cavern 220 ft long and 60 ft high in basalt cliffs. Inspiration for Mendelssohn's "Hebrides" overture. Visit by regular boat from Ulva Ferry (Mull) with connection from Oban, May-Sept, or by arrangement from Iona and elsewhere in Mull.

2 Pass of Brander
A dramatic steep-sided defile at the west foot of Ben Cruachan through which pass the Glasgow-Oban road and railway.

3 Pulpit Hill, Oban
Views over Firth of Lorn and Sound of Mull.

🎦 MUSEUMS

1 Oban Museum
Open Mon-Fri, 10 am to 12.30 pm; 2 pm to 4.30 pm; except Tues, 10 am to 12 noon. Entry fee charged.

☆ OTHER PLACES OF INTEREST

1 Clachan Bridge, Isle of Seil
Built in 1791, links island to mainland and is described as the 'Bridge over the Atlantic'.

2 Glassworks, Oban
Glassblowing can be watched, Mon-Fri. No entry fee charged.

3 Inverliever Forest Information Centre
Entry fee charged. (FC). (See also FORESTS).

4 Mull Little Theatre, Dervaig
See posters or enquire locally.

2 Tweed Mill, Oban
Exhibit on the making of woollen cloth. No entry fee charged.

✿ GARDENS

1 Achnacloich
Spring bulbs, woodland and shrubs. Open Apr-May, Mon-Fri.

2 An Cala, Easdale
Garden on island of Seil featuring cherries, roses and azaleas, rock and water gardens. Open, Apr-Sept, Thurs pm only.

3 Ardanaseig
Rare shrubs and trees and rhododendrons. Open, 10 am to 6 pm, late Mar-Sept.

4 Ardchattan Priory
Open daily

5 Arduaine Gardens
Noted for magnolias, rhododendrons, azaleas and rare trees and shrubs.

6 Barguillean, Glen Lonan
Woodland garden in process of creation and extension.

7 Calgary House, Mull
Island garden with flowering shrubs. Open daily 10 am to 5 pm, late Mar-Sept.

8 Torosay Castle Gardens
Open, May-Sept.

ℹ TOURIST INFORMATION CENTRES

1 Oban
Argyll Square. Tel: 0631 3122 or 3551.

2 Tobermory (S)
Tel: 0688 2182.

FORESTS

Barcaldine Forest
Three walks with car parks and two picnic places. All year. Walks: Craigneuk NM 905377; Glen Dubh NM 966424; Eas na Circe NM 996440 (all on A828, Connel — Ballachulish Road). Picnic places: St Columba's Bay NM 947414; Sutherland's Grove NM 966424; both on A828.

Mull Forest
Picnic area and walks, Tobermory (FC). Picnic area at Fishnish Bay; cliff walks at Glengorm (Glengorm Estate and FC).

NATIONAL NATURE RESERVES

1 Glasdrum Wood
An ash-hazel wood. Permission required to visit (NCC).

2 Glen Nant
An oak and birch wood. (NCC).

NATIONAL TRUST FOR SCOTLAND ESTATES

1 Burg, Isle of Mull
2000 acres on north side of Loch Scridain. A fossil tree possibly 50 million years old can be reached at low water. Cars inadvisable beyond Tiroran. (NTS).

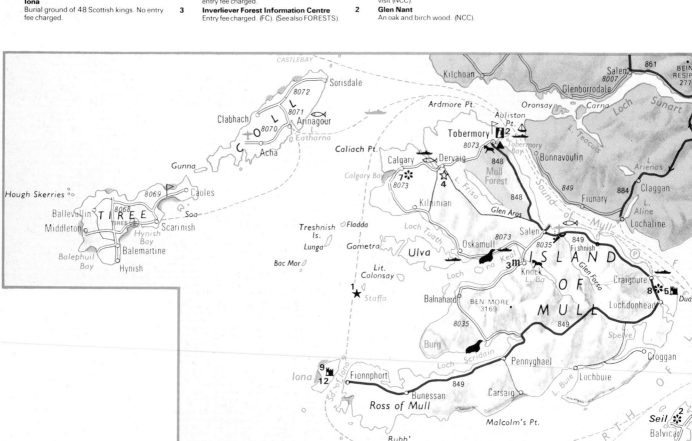

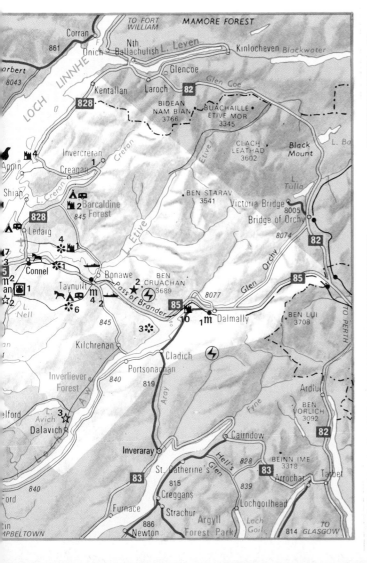

BUILDINGS AND CASTLES

1 Achnacarry Castle
Ancestral home of Clan Cameron and used as Commando training HQ during Second World War. Not open to public.

2 Castle Tioram
Remains of 14th C fortress of the MacDonalds of Clanranald destroyed in 1715. On island in Loch Moidart linked to mainland in all but extreme tides. No entry fee charged.

3 Invergarry Castle
Burned by the Duke of Cumberland after the Battle of Culloden. No entry fee charged. In private grounds of Glengarry Castle Hotel.

4 Inverlochy Castle
Built in 13th C, now ruined, but being restored. Scene of famous battle between Montrose and Argyll in 1645. (AM). Not open to public — view from outside.

5 Kinlochaline Castle
Ancient tower at Loch Aline associated with Clan Macinnes. No entry fee charged.

6 Kinloch Castle, Rhum
In possession of Nature Conservancy Council, occasionally open to public by special cruises from Mallaig.

7 Mingary Castle, Ardnamurchan
A ruined but well preserved castle near Mingary Pier. No entry fee charged.

8 St. Andrew's Church, Fort William
Built 1880, the church is reputed to be one of the most beautiful in Scotland.

MONUMENTS AND SITES

1 Ballachulish Monument
Commemorates the wrongful execution of James Stewart for the murder of Colin Campbell — 'The Red Fox'.

2 Commando Memorial, Spean Bridge
Designed by Scott Sutherland and erected in 1952 to mark the area in which the Commandos were trained during the Second World War.

3 Glencoe Memorial
Monument to the murdered MacDonald chief in the massacre of Glencoe in 1692.

4 Glenfinnan
Monument erected in 1815 to commemorate the raising of Prince Charles' standard in August 1745 as a rallying point for his followers. (NTS). (See also OTHER PLACES OF INTEREST).

5 Well of the Seven Heads, Loch Oich
Monument commemorating the slaying of a father and his six sons for the murder of the heir of the Chief of Keppoch and his brothers.

★ GEOGRAPHICAL FEATURES

1 Ardnamurchan Point
Most westerly point of the British mainland. Name means 'Cape of the Great Seas'.

2 Ben Nevis
Highest peak in Britain at 4418 ft. (1344m). Easiest access by pony track from Achintee. Safe in summer only when clear of snow.

3 Caledonian Canal
Built by Thomas Telford and opened in 1847. Links the lochs in the Great Glen.

4 Camus Musical Sands
In a bay in the north of Eigg the sands make their shrill music when dry and blown by wind. Visit by cruise launches from Mallaig and Arisaig.

5 Dark Mile of Trees, Achnacarry
Remnants of once magnificent avenue of trees.

6 Sgurr of Eigg
1280 ft. high hill of pitchstone. Unusually shaped with hexagonal columns overlying levels of conglomerate and basalt.

 MUSEUMS

1 West Highlands Museum, Fort William
Relics of the '45.

2 Glencoe and North Lorn Folk Museum
MacDonald and Jacobite relics. Open May-Sept., 10 a.m. to 5.30 p.m. (later July and Aug.). Entry fee charged.

☆ OTHER PLACES OF INTEREST

1 Glenfinnan Viaduct
Completed in 1901 by Robert 'Concrete Bob' MacAlpine as part of the railway line to Mallaig, it was the largest poured concrete structure of its time.

2 Road to the Isles (A830)
Scenic road through Glenfinnan, Arisaig and Morar to Mallaig and Skye.

Glengarry Forest
Forest trail and picnic area in the Garry gorge. (FC).

Glenhurich
Picnic place and viewpoint for Loch Doilet. (FC).

Glenrigh Forest
Inchree picnic place and waterfall walk. (FC). Loch Linnhe picnic place. (FC).

NATIONAL NATURE RESERVES

1 Arriundle Oakwood
Semi-natural oakwood with rich carpet of mosses and liverworts. Strontian Glen Nature Trail along track through wood to lead mines. Leaflet at Strontian village centre. (NCC).

2 Glen Roy
A unique British example of late-glacial lake terraces. Viewpoint at car park at entrance to reserve. (NCC).

3 Rhum
A spectacular island of high mountains which has housed a major red deer research project. Kinloch Castle. Kinloch Glen and South Side Nature Trail. Permission required to visit parts of reserve away from Loch Scresort area. (NCC).

3 Visitors Centre, Glencoe
Open mid-May to mid-Oct; Mon-Sat, 10 a.m. to 6 p.m.; Sun 2 p.m. to 6 p.m. Entry fee charged. (See also NATIONAL TRUST FOR SCOTLAND ESTATES)

4 Visitor Centre, Glenfinnan
Entry fee charged. (See also MONUMENTS AND SITES).

TOURIST INFORMATION CENTRES

1 Fort William
Cameron Square. Tel: 0397 2466.

2 Glencoe (S). Tel: Ballachulish 08552 296.

3 Mallaig (S). Tel: 0687 2170.

FOREST

Fort William area
Walks through many of the Lochaber forests. Map available locally. (FC).

Glencoe Forest
Caravan and camping site NN 112576. (A82 Tyndrum-Fort William road). Signal Rock and Lochan Forest Trails NN 121564 and NN 105590 from A82. Booklet from camp site and local shop.

NATIONAL TRUST FOR SCOTLAND ESTATES

1 Glencoe and Dalness
14,200 acres of climbing and walking country. Noted for wildlife and flora. (NTS). (See also OTHER PLACES OF INTEREST).

CHAIRLIFT

1 White Corries, Glencoe
Operative May-Sept., 10 a.m. to 5 p.m., Mon-Sat. Entry fee charged.

Inverness, Loch Ness and Nairn
Spey Valley
Easter Ross and Black Isle

BUILDINGS AND CASTLES

Inverness, Loch Ness and Nairn

1 **Abertarff House, Inverness**
16th C house, probably the oldest in Inverness, with turnpike staircase. Now leased to An Comunn Gaidhealach. (NTS). No entry fee charged. Open normal office hours, Mon-Fri. (See also OTHER PLACES OF INTEREST).

2 **Ardclach Belltower**
14 ft square, two-storey tower dated 1655 used to summon worshippers to nearby Ardclach Church and also to give warning in times of alarm. Admission standard, apply key keeper. (AM).

3 **Beauly Priory**
One of three monastic houses of the Valliscaulian Order founded in Scotland in 1230. Only the church remains. (AM). Entry fee charged.

4 **Boath Doocot, Auldearn**
17th C doocot on site of ancient castle. Montrose flew standard of Charles I here when he defeated the Covenanters in 1645. Battle plan on display. Doocot viewed from outside only. (NTS).

5 **Cawdor Castle**
Seat of the Earl of Cawdor dating from the 15th C standing in wooded grounds. Open daily, June 1-Sept 8, 10 am to 5.30 pm. Entry fee charged. (See also GARDENS).

1 **Cromwell's Clock Tower, Inverness**
All that remains of the Citadel built between 1652 and 1657 by Cromwell's troops, and later destroyed by local people. View from outside only.

1 **Dunbar's Hospital, Inverness**
Alms house built in 1688 with stone taken from the destroyed Citadel. Now old people's rest rooms. Free to OAP's. Open Mon-Fri, 10 am to 5 pm; Sat, 1 pm to 5 pm.

6 **Fort George**
18th C barracks and fortress built after the 45 and still in use. (AM). Entry fee charged. Open, April-Sept (exc 15-29 June), Mon-Sat, 10 am to 6.30 pm; Sun, 2 pm to 6.30 pm.

1 **Inverness Castle**
Built early 19th C on site of castle destroyed in 1746. Monument to Flora MacDonald on Esplanade. Now used as courthouse: view from outside only.

7 **Kilravock Castle**
Home of the Rose family since the 13th C, the present building dates from 1460. Open to the public by prior arrangement — Wed 4 pm. Tea and tour of Castle. Tel: Croy 258.

8 **Rait Castle**
Remains of the ancient seat of the Mackintoshes of Rait, dating from 13th C. View from outside only.

1 **St Andrew's Cathedral, Inverness**
Built 1866-71 and attractively sited by the River Ness.

9 **St Benedict's Abbey, Fort Augustus**
Built in 19th C on site of the old fort constructed after the 1715 rising. Now houses a boys' school run by Benedictine monks.

1 **Town House, Inverness**
Gothic style building containing many fine paintings and a document of the 1921 Cabinet Meeting held there. Open Mon-Fri, normal office hours. No entry fee.

10 **Urquhart Castle, Drumnadrochit**
Overlooking Loch Ness the ruined castle occupies the site of a vitrified fort. Most of the existing building dates from 1509. Entry fee charged. (AM).

Spey Valley

11 **Castle Grant, nr Grantown-on-Spey**
Home of the Chiefs of Clan Grant for over 600 years. Present building dates from 1536. Not open to public.

12 **Castle Roy, near Nethybridge**
Built in 12th or 13th C. Remains beside Abernethy Church on B970. No entry fee charged.

13 **Insh Church**
18th C church with 8th C Celtic bell, built on site used for Christian worship since 6th C.

14 **Loch-an-Eilean**
On an island in the loch are ruins of a fortress supposedly used by the notorious Wolf of Badenoch in the late 14th C. View from shore only.

15 **Ruthven Barracks**
Remains of barracks built in 1719, captured and burned by Jacobites in 1746. (AM).

East Ross and Black Isle

16 **Croick Church**
Inscriptions on windows by persons sheltering in churchyard after the 'Clearances'.

17 **Fearn Abbey**
Founded in 13th C and still partly in use.

18 **Fortrose Cathedral and Precincts**
Remaining portions are complete with 14th C detail to be seen. (AM).

19 **Foulis Castle, Evanton**
Seat of Munro family, rebuilt in 18th C. Private residence, but members of Clan Munro may be received by making private appointment.

20 **St Duthus Chapel, Tain**
Ruins of 13th C chapel with fine stained glass windows.

21 **Strathpeffer Pump Room**
Remnant of former Spa days. Pump Room in full working order with mineral waters on tap.

MONUMENTS AND SITES

Inverness, Loch Ness and Nairn

1 **Boar Stone, Inverness**
Sculptured stone believed to date from Pictish times.

2 **Clava Cairns**
Late Neolithic or early Bronze Age chambered cairns with associated standing stone circles. (AM).

3 **Cobb Memorial, Loch Ness**
Monument to John Cobb, killed on the loch while making a world water speed record attempt.

4 **Corriemony Chambered Cairn, Glenurquhart**
Neolithic passage grave in roughly circular mound, 16 ft in diameter and 8 ft high with associated standing stones. (AM).

5 **Culloden Battlefield, Nr Inverness**
Scene of the defeat in 1746 of Prince Charles by the Duke of Cumberland. Graves of the clans, 'Well of the Dead'. (NTS). Car parks and walks. (FC). (See also MUSEUMS).

6 **Well of St Ignatius, Beauly**
Built in 1800 and rebuilt in 1955 to commemorate the Coronation. The stone is carved with names, dates and symbols.

Spey Valley

7 **Aviemore**
Burial cairn estimated at 1500 BC. Beside fire station at north end of village. No entry fee charged.

8 **Loch Einich and Loch Morlich**
Remains of weirs used when logs from the pine forests of Abernethy, Glenmore and Rothiemurchus were floated down the Spey and its tributaries to serve the boatbuilding industries which flourished at the mouth of the river between 1783 and 1890. Loch Morlich — 8 miles from Aviemore on A951. Loch Einich — track from Coylumbridge.

9 **Norwegian Commandos Memorial**
Memorial stone to 'linge' company who trained in Cairngorm area. By Glenmore Information Office.

10 **War Memorial, nr Kingussie**
Witch of Laggan reported to have been burnt to death here about 200 years ago. Calcified human remains were found while building war memorial in 1920.

East Ross and Black Isle

11 **Chanonry Point**
Supposedly the site of the death of the Brahan Seer 'in a spiked barrel of boiling tar'. (See also BIRD SANCTUARIES AND OBSERVATION POINTS).

12 **Eagle Stone, Strathpeffer**
Stone with horseshoe pattern and carved eagle featured in one of Braham Seer's prophecies.

13 **Sir Hector MacDonald Monuments, Dingwall and Mulbuie**
Monuments to a local boy who rose from the ranks to General.

14 **Tolbooth, Tain**
Mediaeval type tower housing the curfew bell. Below it is the Mercat Cross.

GEOGRAPHICAL FEATURES

Inverness, Loch Ness and Nairn

Caledonian Canal
Built by Thomas Telford and opened in 1847. Links the lochs in the Great Glen.

1 **Falls of Foyers**
On east side of Loch Ness. Upper fall is 30 ft and lower 90 ft. Care needed.

2 **Loch Ness**
Fresh water loch 21¾ miles long and over 900 ft deep in the major geological fault known as the Great Glen. Home of the legendary monster!

3 **Ness Islands, Inverness**
Wooded islands on River Ness near town centre linked by footbridges.

Spey Valley

4 **Lairig Ghru**
An ancient right of way and pass, 25 miles long, from Speyside to Deeside.

5 **Loch Insh**
Interest to bird watchers.

6 **Loch Morlich**
Beautiful inland loch in Glenmore Forest Park at altitude of 1046 ft.

East Ross and Black Isle

7 **Ben Wyvis**
3,433 ft mountain. Easiest access by forestry road from Garbat. Care needed.

8 **Black Rock Gorge, Evanton**
Reached by a path to the west of the town.

9 **Eathie Burn, Black Isle**
Site of researches by Hugh Miller. Fossils may be found in carboniferous shale on foreshore.

10 **Falls of Rogie**
Waterfall near roadside of Muir of Ord/Garve Road.

11 **Struie Hill**
Viewpoint offers panoramic views east and west over the Dornoch Firth.

MUSEUMS

Inverness, Loch Ness and Nairn

1 **Inverness Museum**
Open, Mon-Sat, 9 am to 5 pm. No entry fee charged.

2 **Leanach Cottage Museum and Culloden Visitor Centre**
On Culloden Battlefield (NTS). Open mid-April-October 31, 9.30 am to 6 pm; except 1 June-31 August, 9.30 am to 9.30 pm; Sun, 2 pm to 6.30 pm. Entry fee charged. (See also MONUMENTS AND SITES).

Spey Valley

3 **Am Fasgach Folk Museum, Kingussie**
Highland Folk Museum. Record of old Highland life and social development.

4 **Boat of Garten Museum**

5 **Clan MacPherson House, Newtonmore**
Portraits, documents and other relics of clan including the celebrated black chanter of the clan battle at Perth. Open weekdays and Saturdays, 10 am to 12 noon, 2 pm to 6 pm.

East Ross and Black Isle

6 **Dingwall Museum**
Town Hall, Dingwall. Open — Mon-Sat, 11 am to 1 pm; 2 pm to 4 pm. Mainly historical collections connected with surrounding area. Advance notice required for bus parties.

7 **Hugh Miller's Cottage, Cromarty**
Birthplace, dating from 1650, of Hugh Miller (1802-56) — geologist, naturalist, theologian and writer. Now a museum dedicated to him. (NTS). Open: Apr-Oct, 10 am to 12 noon; 1 pm to 5 pm; Sun, 2 pm to 5 pm June-Sep only. Entry fee charged.

OTHER PLACES OF INTEREST

Inverness, Loch Ness and Nairn

1 **Abertarff House, Inverness**
Headquarters of An Comunn Gaidhealach (The Highland Association) with information centre. No entry fee charged. Open normal office hours, Mon-Fri. (See also BUILDINGS AND CASTLES).

1 **Eden Court Theatre Complex**
No entry fee except for Theatre. For programmes see local press and publicity.

2 **Farigaig Forest Centre**
(FC). (See also FORESTS).

3 **Great Glen Exhibition, Fort Augustus**

1 **Inverness Ice Rink**
Open daily, 2.30 pm to 5 pm, 6.30 pm to 9 pm. Entry fee charged. (Skate hire).

Spey Valley

4 **Aviemore Holiday Centre**
Swimming pool, ice rink, theatre/cinema, ballroom, children's play area, restaurants and shops. Dry ski-slope, go-karting and nature trail.

5 **Carrbridge Visitors Centre — 'Landmark'**
Multi-screen auditorium depicting 100 centuries of Highland history. Exhibition, restaurant and shop. Picnic area and nature trail.

6 **Glenmore Information Centre**
Entry Fee charged. (FC). (See also FOREST PARKS).

7 **Highland Wildlife Park, Kincraig**
The wildlife of the Highlands in their natural habitat. Drive-through section, children's section, etc. Open 10 am to 6 pm (or 1½ hours before dusk, if earlier). Entry fee charged.

5 **Old Bridge of Carr, Carrbridge**
Remains of original stone bridge built about 1717.

8 **Reindeer Herd**
Visits to reindeer herd. Depart 11 am from Reindeer House, nr Glenmore Camp Site. Fee charged.

9 **Strathspey Steam Railway**
Nine 'steam days' at weekends throughout holiday season.

10 **Visitors Centre, Loch-an-Eilean**
Open, May-Sept. (NCC). (See also NATIONAL NATURE RESERVES).

East Ross and Black Isle

11 **Dingwall Swimming Pool and Sports Centre**
During school term, pool open to public Mon-Fri, 1 pm to 2 pm and evenings only; except Wed — 1 pm to 2 pm only; Sat, 9 am to 12.45 pm; 2.15 pm to 4.30 pm; Sun, 8 am to 11 am; 2 pm to 4 pm. During school holidays, open 9 am till evening. Games hall can be hired with games equipment.

12 **Fish Lift, Torr Achilty**
Open June-Oct. Visit 9 am to 11 am; 3 pm to 4 pm.

GARDENS

Inverness, Loch Ness and Nairn

1 **Bellfield Park, Inverness**
Public gardens with associated recreational facilities.

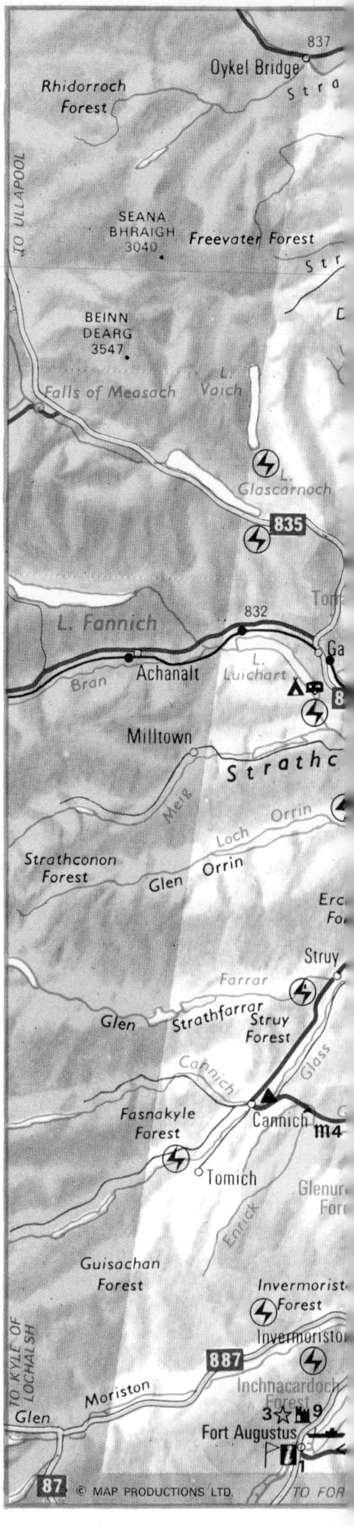

2 **Cawdor Castle Gardens**
Formal gardens and wooded garden on banks of Cawdor burn. (Castle and gardens); open daily, June 1-Sept 8, 10 am to 5.30 pm. Entry fee charged (See also BUILDINGS AND CASTLES).

3 **Viewfield House, Nairn**
Small public garden with rockeries and well in grounds of museum.

Spey Valley

4 **Inshriach Rock Garden**
Commercial grower of Alpine rock plants. No entry fee charged.

5 **Speyside Heather Centre, Dulnain Bridge**
Garden teas.

East Ross and Black Isle

6 **'900 Roses' Garden, Tain**
Garden laid out to celebrate the 900th anniversary of the burgh receiving it's Royal Charter.

BIRD SANCTUARIES AND OBSERVATION POINTS

Inverness, Loch Ness and Nairn

1 **Longman Bay, Inverness**
Waders, ducks and gulls.

Spey Valley

2 Loch Garten
Observation post for ospreys, open April-Sept when ospreys present: 1500 acre pinewoods reserve, crested tits, crossbills, red squirrels. (RSPB) Insh marshes RSPB reserve. Loch Insh.

East Ross and Black Isle

5 Beauly Firth
Waders and wildfowl, especially goosanders in winter and Canadian geese in summer.

4 Chanonry Point
Migration point. (See also MONUMENTS AND SITES).

5 Munlochy Bay
Wintering flock of ducks, waders and geese. (LNR).

6 Nigg Bay
Waders and ducks, especially wigeon.

7 Rosemarkie
Fulmar colony, pinkfeet in spring.

8 Tarbat Ness
Observation point for migration. Eider duck, common and velvet scoters in winter.

9 Udale Bay
Ducks, waders, curlew, bar-tailed godwit and dunlin.

TOURIST INFORMATION CENTRES

Inverness, Loch Ness and Nairn

1 Fort Augustus (S)
Tel: 03203 367.

2 Inverness
Church Street. Tel: 0463 34353.

3 Nairn (S)
Tel: 95 52753.

Spey Valley

4 Aviemore
Grampian Road. Tel: Aviemore 047 981 363.

5 Grantown on Spey (S)
Tel: Grantown on Spey 047 9 2773.

6 Newtonmore (S)
Tel: Newtonmore 05403 253.

East Ross and Black Isle

7 Muir of Ord
Information Centre. Tel: Muir of Ord 82 433

8 Strathpeffer (S)
Tel: Strathpeffer 94415.

9 Tarvie (S)
Tel: Strathpeffer 94575.

FORESTS

Inverness, Loch Ness and Nairn

Craig Phadrig Forest
Forest walk leading to vitrified fort and forestry research plots. Leaflet (FC).

Culloden Forest
Forest trail through interesting mixed woodland. Guide book (FC).

Culloden Moor
Picnic place and battlefield walk (FC). (See also MUSEUMS).

Farigaig Forest
Forest trail through mixed woodland of mature conifers and native broadleaved trees. Information centre, picnic area, guide book. (FC). (See also OTHER PLACES OF INTEREST).

Glenurquhart Forest
Forest walk (FC).

Inchnacardoch Forest
Forest trails through Scotland's first state forest. Picnic places. Guide book (FC).

Reelig Glen Forest
Forest walks through wooded glens of Douglas Fir. Of geological, botanical and archaeological interest. Guide book (FC).

Spey Valley

Inshriach Forest
Forest walk at Rockwood Ponds (FC). Picnic places at Tolvah, Feshiebridge and Rockwood Ponds (FC).

Queen's Forest
(See under Glen More Forest Park).

East Ross and Black Isle

Torrachilty Forest
Forest walks and picnic places. NH/442583 on A832 Contin-Garve road. Paths to Rogie Falls. Picnic area. NH/396630 — picnic area on A835 Garve-Ullapool road one mile north of Garve, on Blackwater river side. NH/195807, on A835, 9 miles south-east of Ullapool — Forest walk, forest garden, picnic area, guide book. NH/455568, 6 miles west of Dingwall at Contin on A834 — forest walk, guide book.

FOREST PARKS

Spey Valley

Glen More Forest Park
6500 acres of woodland and of high ground including Loch Morlich, Queen's Forest and remnants of old Caledonian pine forests. The park offers a wide range of leisure activities including climbing, canoeing, fishing and sailing. Information centre, camp site, picnic area, hostel, shop, forest walks. Guide book. (FC). (See also OTHER PLACES OF INTEREST.)

NATIONAL NATURE RESERVES

Spey Valley

Cairngorms
Largest reserve in Britain, noted for wildlife. Chairlift to Cairngorm mountain. Loch an Eilein and Achlean Nature Trails open all year. Access restricted to parts of reserve in late summer and autumn. (NCC). (See also OTHER PLACES OF INTEREST.)

Craigellachie
Stand of pure birchwood and moorland. Birchwood Nature Trail open all year. (NCC).

CHAIRLIFTS

Spey Valley

1 Car Park, Cairngorm
Adm: None

1 Coire na Ciste, Cairngorm
Adm: Winter — ski-ing tickets available — weekly, daily, ½ day.

Ptarmigan Restaurant
At top of chairlift. Commands views of Strathspey.

1 West Wall, Coire na Ciste
Adm: Summer and winter prices — unable to quote as new prices awaited.

1 White Lady, Cairngorm
Adm: Winter — ski-ing tickets available — weekly, daily, ½ day.

BUILDINGS AND CASTLES

Wester Ross

1 **Bernera Barracks, Glenelg**
One of a chain built across the Highlands after the risings of 1715 and 1745.

2 **Eilean Donan Castle, nr Dornie**
Built in 1220 and blown up in 1719 by an English man o' war. Rebuilt 1912-1930.

3 **Strome Castle**
Mediaeval castle destroyed in 1609 by English troops after a long siege. (NTS).

Skye

4 **Armadale Castle**
Home of the MacDonald's of Sleat. Accessible at all times. Collection box.

5 **Castle Macil, Kyleakin**
Ruined castle overlooking ferry crossing to Skye. Supposedly built by Norwegian princess to exort tolls from ships using the strait. Accessible at all times. No entry fee charged.

6 **Dunscaith Castle, Tarskavaig**
Once stronghold of chiefs of Macdonald. Now a ruin. Accessible at all times. No entry fee charged.

7 **Duntulm Castle**
Ancient seat of the Macdonalds of the Isles. No entry fee charged.

8 **Dunvegan Castle**
Home of the chiefs of the Clan MacLeod since about 1200 and famed for 'Fairy Flag' and Bottle Dungeon. Boat trips to Seal Islands. Open daily except Sun: (Easter-June) 2 pm to 5 pm; (July-Aug) 10.30 am to 5 pm. (Sept-Oct) 2 pm to 5 pm. Entry fee charged.

9 **Raasay House**
Fine building now derelict. Dr Johnson stayed here on tour of Hebrides in 1773. Visit by boat from Portree. Not open to public — view from outside.

MONUMENTS AND SITES

Wester Ross

1 **Dun Lagaidh**
Iron Age fort and broch on SW shore of Loch Broom.

© MAP PRODUCTIONS LTD.

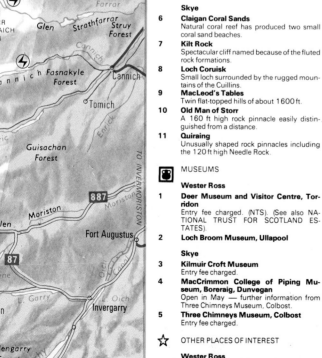

2 Glenelg Brochs
Two Iron Age brochs over 30 ft high with well-preserved features. (AM).

3 Totaig Broch, Loch Duich
Iron Age broch, still standing 13 ft high with wall-chambers and part of staircase and gallery still evident.

Skye

4 Beinn na Caillich
Cairn on top of mountain said to mark grave of 13th C Norwegian princess.

5 Dun Fiadhairt
Iron Age broch about 12 ft thick and 31 ft in diameter.

6 Dun Hallin
Iron Age broch still over 12 ft high within a 6 ft thick enclosing wall. Accessible at all times. No entry fee charged.

7 Kilmuir
Burial place of Flora MacDonald, who died in 1790. Original tombstone has been replaced by Celtic cross. Accessible at all times. No entry fee charged.

8 Rubh'an Dunain
Iron Age dun of 'galleried' type and Neolithic chambered cairn. Accessible at all times. No entry fee charged.

★ **GEOGRAPHICAL FEATURES**

Wester Ross

1 Bealach nam Bo (Pass of the Cattle)
Pass from Tornapress to Applecross reaches 2054 ft at the summit with hairpin bends and fine views.

2 Corrieshalloch Gorge
Mile-long gorge 200 ft deep with suspension bridge to view 150 ft Falls of Measach. (NTS/NCC).

3 Falls of Glomach
370 ft high waterfall reached by Kililan or Morvich. Care needed. (NTS).

4 Loch Hourn
Fjord-like inlet flanked by sheer rocky walls. View from Sgurr a Mhaoraich.

5 Mam Ratagan
1116 ft high pass on road to Glenelg. View over Loch Duich from summit.

Skye

6 Claigan Coral Sands
Natural coral reef has produced two small coral sand beaches.

7 Kilt Rock
Spectacular cliff named because of the fluted rock formations.

8 Loch Coruisk
Small loch surrounded by the rugged mountains of the Cuillins.

9 MacLeod's Tables
Twin flat-topped hills of about 1600 ft.

10 Old Man of Storr
A 160 ft high rock pinnacle easily distinguished from a distance.

11 Quiraing
Unusually shaped rock pinnacles including the 120 ft high Needle Rock.

▣ **MUSEUMS**

Wester Ross

1 Deer Museum and Visitor Centre, Torridon
Entry fee charged. (NTS). (See also NATIONAL TRUST FOR SCOTLAND ESTATES).

2 Loch Broom Museum, Ullapool

Skye

3 Kilmuir Croft Museum
Entry fee charged.

4 MacCrimmon College of Piping Museum, Boreraig, Dunvegan
Open in May — further information from Three Chimneys Museum, Colbost.

5 Three Chimneys Museum, Colbost
Entry fee charged.

☆ **OTHER PLACES OF INTEREST**

Wester Ross

1 Ardessie Falls
Dundonnell, Loch Broom.

2 Aultroy Visitors Centre
Open: mid-May to mid-September. (NCC). (See also NATIONAL NATURE RESERVES).

3 Caves
Gruinard Bay, Loch Ewe and South Erradale (Gairloch). Those at Sand of Udrigle and Cove formerly were used as places of worship.

4 Inverewe Gardens Visitors Centre

5 Knockam Visitors Centre
Open mid-May to mid-Sept (NCC). (See also NATIONAL NATURE RESERVES).

6 Visitors Centre, Balmacara
Open — June-Sept, 10 am to 1 pm and 2 pm to 6 pm; Sun 2 pm to 6 pm (NTS). (See also NATIONAL TRUST FOR SCOTLAND ESTATES).

7 Visitors Centre, Morvich Camping Site
Audio-visual exhibition. Entry fee charged. (NTS).

Skye

8 Drynoch Bridge
Spans a burn leading to Loch Harport and said to be the highest masonry bridge in Scotland.

9 Fairy Bridge, Dunvegan Road
On this bridge the Fairy Flag was handed to one of the Chiefs of Clan MacLeod and can now be seen in Dunvegan Castle.

10 Neist Point Lighthouse, Glendale
No entry fee charged.

11 Sabhal Mhor, Ostaig, Sleat
College of Gaelic offering classes for Gaelic language summer courses — bookings in advance.

12 Talisker Distillery, Carbost
Conducted tours available free of charge throughout tourist season at 11 am and 3 pm.

13 Trumpan Churchyard, Waternish
Ruins of church and graveyard. Open at all times. No entry fee charged.

✱ **GARDENS**

Wester Ross

1 Dundonnell House
Private gardens with rare oriental shrubs and aviaries of exotic birds. Occasionally open to public.

2 Inverewe Gardens
Semi-tropical gardens containing many rare and unusual plants, begun in 1865 by Osgood Mackenzie. (NTS). Open — dawn to dusk; entry fee charged. Restaurant — standard, Apr-Sept. (See also OTHER PLACES OF INTEREST).

3 Lael Forest Garden, nr Ullapool
Garden containing some 150 different trees and shrubs. Entry fee charged (FC). (See also FORESTS).

🐦 **BIRD SANCTUARIES AND OBSERVATION POINTS**

Skye

1 Ascrib Islands
Puffins

ℹ **TOURIST INFORMATION CENTRES**

Wester Ross

1 Gairloch
Sands Holiday Centre. Tel: 0445 2139.

2 Kyle of Lochalsh (S)
Tel: 0599 4276.

3 Ullapool (S)
Tel: 0854 2135.

Skye

4 Broadford (S)

5 Portree
Meall House. Tel: 0478 2137. Oldest building in Portree, was once the old jailhouse: original domed ceilings can still be seen.

FORESTS 57

Wester Ross

Glen Affric
Forest trails, walks and picnic areas in superb Highland scenery.

Lael Forest
Forest walk with views of Loch Broom. Includes Lael Forest Garden. Leaflet. (FC). (See also GARDENS).

Ratagan Forest
Doruisduian picnic place. Car park for Falls of Glomach walk. (FC).

Slattadale Forest
Forest trails, picnic area on shores of Loch Maree. Leaflet (FC).

Skye

Skye Forest
Forest walks and viewpoints, Glenuarragill, Portree (FC). Viewpoint car park, Glenbrittle (FC).

NATIONAL NATURE RESERVES

Wester Ross

1 Allt nan Carnan
Mile long gorge, 80 feet deep, in which oak and birch dominate. (NCC).

2 Beinn Eighe
Contains large remnant of Caledonian forest and many rare animals such as the pine marten. Glas Leitire Nature Trail and Beinn Eighe Mountain Trail. (NCC). (See also OTHER PLACES OF INTEREST).

3 Corrieshalloch
Wooded gorge, a mile long and 200 feet deep with the 150 feet Falls of Measach. (NCC).

4 Inverpolly
Lewisian gneiss glaciated plateau with Torridonian sandstone mountains. Wild and remote area of 26,827 acres. Remnant woodlands. Wildlife includes wildcat, pine marten, eagle, etc. Knockan Cliff Nature Trail and Geological Trail. Permission required to visit Drumrunie late summer and autumn. (NCC). (See also OTHER PLACES OF INTEREST).

5 Rassal Ashwood
An ashwood with limestone outcrop. (NCC).

SCOTTISH WILDLIFE TRUST RESERVES

Wester Ross

1 Eilean na Creige Duibhe
In Plockton Bay, some 150-200 yards offshore. Herons and otters. Access by boat from Plockton (SWT). Please observe notices.

NATIONAL TRUST FOR SCOTLAND ESTATES

Wester Ross

1 Balmacara Estate
6,400 acres covering most of Kyle/Plockton peninsula. (NTS). (See also OTHER PLACES OF INTEREST).

2 Kintail
12,800 acres of magnificent scenery including the Five Sisters of Kintail. Herds of red deer and wild goats. (NTS).

3 Shieldaig Island
32 acre island in Loch Torridon almost entirely covered with Scots pine. (NTS).

4 Torridon
14,000 acre estate which includes some of Scotland's finest mountain scenery, and of interest to naturalists and geologists. (NTS). (See also MUSEUMS).

BUILDINGS AND CASTLES

1 Chapel, Toe Head
Dates from about 16th C.

2 Church of St Aula (Olaf), Gress
Only Hebridean church dedicated to a Norse saint. Now a ruin.

3 Kismul Castle, Barra
Built on rock in Castlebay in 1030, recently restored by present Macneil of Barra.

4 Lews Castle, Stornoway
Built in 1884, former home of Lord Leverhulme and now a county council college. Surroundings include largest wooded park in Western Isles.

5 St Clement's Church, Rodel
Early 16th C, restored 1873, with sculptured tombs. (AM).

6 St Moluag's Church, Butt of Lewis
Built about 12th C to commemorate a disciple of St Columba. Still in use.

7 Trinity Temple, nr Carnish
Founded in 1203 on foundations of earlier place of worship and later rebuilt.

8 Ui Chapel, Eye Peninsula
Ancient burial ground of the MacLeod chiefs.

MONUMENTS AND SITES

1 Callanish Standing Stones
Cruciform setting of standing stones with associated cairns, dating from about 2000 BC. (AM).

2 Dun Carloway Broch
One of best preserved of Iron Age brochs, still 30 ft high. (AM).

3 Flora MacDonald Cairn, Milton
Commemorates her birth in 1722 and is on site of her birthplace.

4 Norse Grinding Mill, Shawbost
Remains of an ancient meal mill.

5 'Our Lady of the Isles', Reuval Hill
Statue of Madonna and Child built in 1957 by Hugh Lorimer for the local Catholic community.

6 'Thrushell Stone', Ballantrushal
An 18 ft high monolith.

7 Whalebone Arch, Bragar
An archway made from a whale's jawbone. The harpoon which killed the whale hangs from the arch.

GEOGRAPHICAL FEATURES

1 Barra Head
Southernmost point of the Western Isles. Visit by boat from Castlebay.

2 Barra Machair
Large areas of grass-bound sands abutting on white shell-sand beaches. Rich in flowers.

3 Butt of Lewis
Exposed point looking out to the Atlantic.

4 Scolpaig
Nearest point to St Kilda (50 miles away) and noted for natural arches.

MUSEUMS

1 Black House, Arnol
Old croft house kept in original condition. Now a museum displaying equipment and utensils used in the past. Open daily, Mon-Sat, May-Oct. Entry fee charged.

2 Shawbost Folk Museum
A collection of island relics and island interests. Open daily, Mon-Sat, May-Oct. Collection at door.

OTHER PLACES OF INTEREST

1 Nicolson/Lewis Swimming Pool and Sports Centre
During school term, pool is open to the public, 12.15 pm to 1.15 pm; 5 pm to 9 pm. During school holidays, 9 am to 9 pm. Entry fee charged: towels, swimming aids for hire. The games hall can also be hired with games equipment. Entry fee charged for spectators.

BIRD SANCTUARIES AND OBSERVATION POINTS

1 Balranald
Summer wardened reserve for waders, ducks, sea birds (RSPB).

2 Butt of Lewis
Good headland for migration.

3 Loch Bee
Mute swans, wildfowl and waders.

4 Loch Druidibeg
Greylag geese. (NCC). (See also NATIONAL NATURE RESERVES).

5 Melbost Sands
Wildfowl and waders.

6 Mingulay
Fulmars and kittiwakes.

7 Monach Isles
Sea birds.

8 Seilebost and Luskentyre
Waders and shore-birds.

9 Shiant Isles
Sea birds and puffins.

TOURIST INFORMATION CENTRES

1 Castlebay (S)
Tel: Castlebay 08714 336.

2 Lochboisdale (S)
Tel: Lochboisdale 08784 286.

3 Lochmaddy (S)
Tel: Lochmaddy 08763 321.

Stornoway

4 South Beach Quay
Tel: Stornoway 0851 3088.

5 Tarbert (S)
Tel: Harris 0859 2011.

NATIONAL NATURE RESERVES

1 Loch Druidibeg, South Uist
Important breeding ground of greylag goose. Viewing tower. Permission to visit required during bird breeding season. (NCC). (See also BIRD SANCTUARIES AND OBSERVATION POINTS).

2 Monach Isles
Small uninhabited islands. Uncultivated machair. Seals, sea birds. Permission to land required from North Uist Estate, Lochmaddy. (NCC).

NATIONAL TRUST FOR SCOTLAND ESTATES

St Kilda
Group of islands 110 miles from mainland uninhabited since 1930. Sea bird colonies. Visit by expedition on application to NTS. (NTS AND NCC).

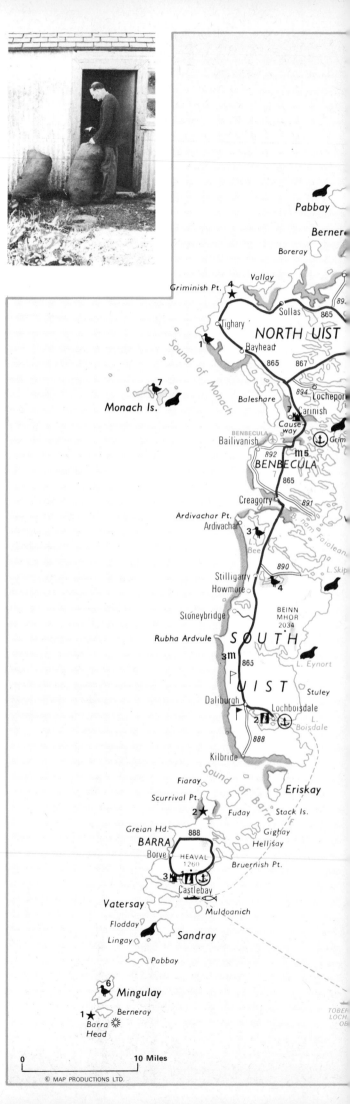

© MAP PRODUCTIONS LTD.

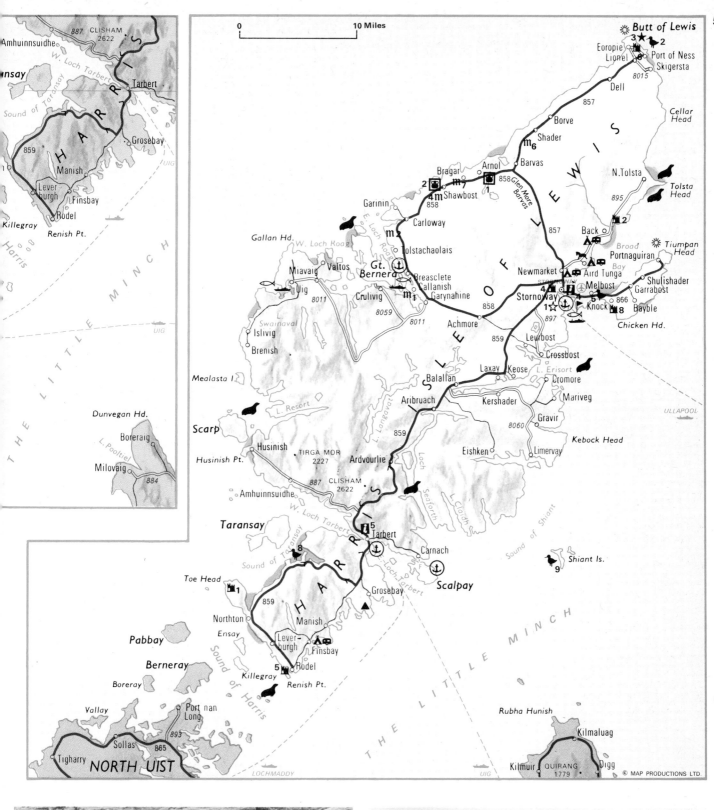

BUILDINGS AND CASTLES

Caithness

1 **Ackergill Tower**
Built about 1591 by MacLeods of Assynt. No entry fee charged.

2 **Bucholie Castle, Freswick**
Ruined, 15th C, former home of the Mowats. No entry fee charged.

3 **Castles Girnigoe and Sinclair, Noss Head**
Castle Girnigoe dates from end of 15th C and Castle Sinclair from early 1/th C. Both ruins. No entry fee charged.

4 **Castle of Mey**
Built in 1570 and now home of Queen Mother. (See also GARDENS).

5 **Castle of Old Wick**
A ruined square tower dating probably from 12th C standing between two arms of the sea. (AM). Closed when adjoining rifle range is in use. No entry fee charged.

6 **Keiss Castle**
Once home of Sir William Sinclair, 17th C founder of first Baptist Church in Scotland at Keiss. No entry fee charged.

7 **Old St. Peter's Church, Thurso**
Founded in 13th C by Bishop of Caithness and in use until 1832. Now roofless. Nave and transept are 16th and 17th C. No entry fee charged.

8 **St. Mary's Chapel, Crosskirk**
Chapel consisting of chancel and nave probably 12th C. Nearby broch remains. (AM).

Sutherland

9 **Ardvreck Castle**
Built on shores of Loch Assynt about 1590, now a ruin. No entry fee charged.

10 **Carbisdale Castle, nr. Invershin**
Built this century for former Dowager Duchess of Sutherland, the castle resembles a Rhine Schloss. Now a youth hostel.

11 **Castle Varrich**
An old square tower, now in ruins, near village of Tongue. No entry fee charged.

12 **Dornoch Castle**
Built in 16th C as residence for Bishops of Caithness. Now a hotel.

12 **Dornoch Cathedral**
13th C Cathedral reconstructed as a parish church in 1835.

13 **Dunrobin Castle, nr. Golspie**
Seat of the Dukes of Sutherland, part of the castle dates to 13th C, but main building is 19th C. Open May-Sept., Mon-Fri, 11 a.m. to 6 p.m.; Sun, 1 p.m. to 6 p.m. Entry fee charged. (See also MUSEUMS and GARDENS).

14 **Skelbo Castle**
Interesting 14th C ruin on shores of Loch Fleet. Not open to public.

15 **Skibo Castle, nr Clashmore**
Modern castle built by Andrew Carnegie at end of 19th C. Now private residence not open to public.

16 **St. Andrew's Church, Golspie**
Early 18th C Church built on site of ancient chapel to St. Andrew the Apostle.

m MONUMENTS AND SITES

Caithness

1 **Cairn of Get**
Neolithic burial chamber in which several skeletons and ornaments were found during excavations in 1866. (AM).

2 **Freswick Bay**
Site of Viking Village.

3 **Grey Cairns of Camster**
Two cairns, the smaller of which is well preserved, dating from about 3000-2000 BC. (AM).

4 **Harold's Tower, Nr Thurso**
Harold, Earl of Caithness, buried here in 1196 and tower built in early 18th C by Sir John Sinclair, the agriculturalist, as a family burial place.

5 **Hill O' Many Stones**
Neolithic or Bronze Age site with almost 200 stones set out in 22 parallel rows. (AM).

6 **Langwell Wag, Berriedale**
Variation of 'wheelhouse' type of Iron Age building thought to be used to protect cattle from wolves.

Sutherland

7 **Dun of Creich, nr Bonar Bridge**
Vitrified fort dating between 200 and 50 BC. No entry fee charged.

8 **Dun Dornadilla**
Pictish broch south of Loch Hope. Open at all times. No entry fee charged.

9 **Earl's Cross, Dornoch**
Monument bearing Arms of Sutherland family and Arms of the Bishop.

10 **Embo**
Neolithic chambered cairn estimated about 1800 BC.

11 **Invernaver, nr Bettyhill**
Cairns, cists, enclosures and hut circles of early date.

12 **Kirkton Farm, nr Golspie**
Remains of early earth houses.

13 **Monument to the Duke of Sutherland**
Statue on top of Ben Bhraggie of the first Duke of Sutherland.

14 **Old Hill, Lairg**
Neolithic chambered cairn excavated in 1967.

15 **Sir John A MacDonald Monument, Rogart**
Marks the birthplace of the first Prime Minister of Canada. Unveiled in 1963 by the then Prime Minister, John Diefenbaker.

16 **Standing Stone, nr Clashmore**
Estimated between 1000 and 500 BC.

17 **Strathsteven Broch, nr Golspie**
Dating from between 200 and 50 BC.

★ GEOGRAPHICAL FEATURES

Caithness

Island of Stroma
In the Pentland Firth, Caithness' only island. Tomb of the Kennedy's and other remains. Difficulty of access due to tides. (This island appears on the Orkney map).

1 **John o' Groats**
Well-known terminal point on mainland.

2 **Merry Men of Mey**
Spectacular tidal race in Pentland Firth. View from St John's Point.

3 **Stacks of Duncansby**
Detached stacks of Old Red Sandstone. (See also BIRD SANCTUARIES AND OBSERVATION POINTS).

Sutherland

4 **Cape Wrath**
Sea cliff of gneiss up to 400 ft high. Visit by ferry and minibus from Durness. (See also BIRD SANCTUARIES).

5 **Clo Mor**
Highest Cliffs on British mainland ranging from 600-900 ft high. (See also BIRD SANCTUARIES).

6 **Inchnadamph Caves**
Limestone caves in which were found bones of late Pleistocene animals and traces of early man. (NCC).

7 **Shin Falls**
Attractive falls famed for salmon leaping.

8 **Smoo Cave, nr Durness**
Three caves in limestone cliffs, two of which are difficult of access.

9 **Waterfall of Eas-Coul-Aulin, Kylesku**
Highest Waterfall in Britain with a drop of 658 ft.

MUSEUMS

Caithness

1 **Folk Museum, Thurso**
Open — June to Sept. No entry fee charged.

1 **Thurso Museum**
Robert Dick Collection. No entry fee charged.

2 **Wick Museum**
Open all year. No entry fee charged.

Sutherland

3 **Dunrobin Castle Museum, nr Golspie**
Entry fee charged. (See also BUILDINGS AND CASTLES and GARDENS).

☆ OTHER PLACES OF INTEREST

Caithness

1 **UKAEA, Dounreay**
Site of nuclear fast reactor and new prototype fast reactor. Observation room. Open May-Sept.

2 **Wick Church of Scotland Exhibition**
Open July and Aug. No entry fee charged.

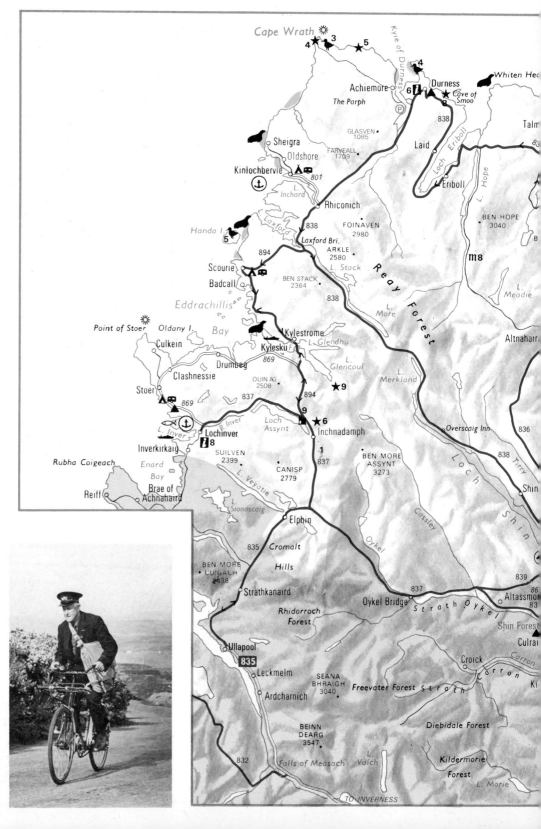

✳ GARDENS

Caithness

1 **Castle of Mey**
Gardens open on only 2 or 3 days in the year — usually one day July, one day Aug.

2 **Langwell, Berriedale**
Fine example of gardening achievement in exposed area. Gardens open on two days usually July / Aug.

Sutherland

3 **Dunrobin Castle Gardens, nr Golspie**
19th C formal gardens laid out in the style of Versailles. (See also BUILDINGS AND CASTLES and MUSEUMS).

4 **Rovie Lodge Gardens, Rogart**
Lawns, heather gardens, water garden and roses.

🐦 BIRD SANCTUARIES AND OBSERVATION POINTS

Caithness

1 **Duncansby Head**
Sea birds.

2 **Dunnet Head**
Sea birds.

Sutherland

3 **Clo Mor and Cape Wrath**
Sea bird colonies and migrants.

4 **Faraid Head and Balnakeil Bay**
Seaducks, puffins and sea bird passage.

5 **Handa Island**
Sea bird colony (RSPB).

ℹ TOURIST INFORMATION CENTRES

Caithness

1 **Thurso** (S)
Riverside Car Park. Tel: 0847 2371.

2 **Wick**
Whitechapel Road. Tel: 0955 2596.

Sutherland

3 **Bonar Bridge** (S)
Tel: Ardgay 08632 333.

4 **Brora**
Tel: 04082 465.

5 **Dornoch**
The Square, Dornoch. Tel: Dornoch 086281 400.

6 **Durness** (S)
Tel: 097181 259.

7 **Lairg** (S) Tel: 0549 2160.

8 **Lochinver** (S)
Tel: 05714 330.

9 **Melvich** (S)
Tel: 06413 255.

FORESTS

Caithness

1 **Rumster**
Picnic area and forest walk. (FC).

Sutherland

2 **Dornoch Forest**
Picnic Place, Skelbo. (FC).

3 **Shin Forest**
Four forest walks with good viewpoints on either side of the Kyles of Sutherland. Picnic area, guide book. (FC).

4 **Tongue Forest**
One of the oldest Forestry Commission woods in Scotland. Forest walk, picnic areas. (FC).

NATIONAL NATURE RESERVES

Sutherland

1 **Inchnadamph**
Limestone area of complex geology, with famous Allt nan Uamh Cave. Limestone flora. Permission required to visit late summer and autumn. (NCC).

2 **Invernaver**
Wide variety of plant habitats including those of blown shell sand. (NCC).

3 **Mound Alderwoods**
Permission required to visit. Alderwood developed on old saltmarsh after the artificial road embankment, known as The Mound, was built across the head of Loch Fleet.

© MAP PRODUCTIONS LTD.

🏰 BUILDINGS AND CASTLES

Orkney

1 Bishop's Palace and Earl Patrick's Palace, Kirkwall
Earl Patrick's Palace started in 1600 is a magnificent but roofless building. Bishop's Palace is 12th C construction with later (16th C) additions. Earl's Palace is the "Most mature and accomplished piece of Renaissance architecture left in Scotland". Admission at standard times. Entry fee charged. (AM).

2 Cubbie Roo's Castle and St Mary's Chapel, Isle of Wyre
Probably earliest stone castle in Scotland dating from 12th C. Chapel dates from late 12 C and is now ruined. Admission at all times. Built by the Viking Kolbein Hruga according to the 'Orkneyinga Saga'. (AM).

3 Italian Chapel, Lamb Holm
Attractive little chapel built by Italian prisoners of war in a Nissen hut. All painting was done free hand, and materials were all scrap. Admission at all times. No entry fee charged.

4 Martello Towers, South Walls
Built for defence during Napoleonic Wars and used in Second World War as radar stations. Most of the 32 British Towers concentrated on South and South East coast of England, built as defences against Napoleon. The two in Orkney were constructed for defence against American privateer vessels. No admission fee charged.

5 Noltland Castle, Westray
Dating from 16th C is finest surviving example of a 'Z-plan' castle. (AM). Admission at all reasonable times on application to Custodian. No entry fee charged.

1 St Magnus Cathedral, Kirkwall
Founded in 1137 and took over 300 years to build. One of the finest and most complete in Scotland. Still used as a place of worship, but owned by the people of Kirkwall through Royal Charter. Church service Sun; open Mon-Sat, 9 am to 1 pm; 2 pm to 5 pm.

6 St Magnus Church, Isle of Egilsay
Dates from end of 12th C and although roofless is almost complete. Admission at all times. Perhaps the most imposing of Orkney's churches after St Magnus Cathedral. (AM).

7 St Nicholas Church, Orphir
The chancel and a small part of the nave remain of this 12th C round church. More commonly referred to as The Round Church, it is a building unique in Scotland, having been modelled on the Church of the Holy Sepulchre in Jerusalem. Built probably by Earl Hakan Paullsan. Admission at all times. No entry fee charged.

Shetland

1 Fort Charlotte, Lerwick
Begun in 1665 to protect the Sound of Bressay against the Dutch, burned by them in 1673 and rebuilt 1781. (AM).

1 Lerwick Town Hall
Scottish Baronial style with stained glass windows and panoramic view from tower. No entry fee charged.

2 Mu Ness Castle, Unst
Late 16th C castle, now in ruins. (AM).

3 Scalloway Castle
Built in 1600 by the notorious Patrick Stewart, Earl of Orkney, in the mediaeval style. (AM) No entry fee charged.

ᛗ MONUMENTS AND SITES

Orkney

1 Broch of Gurness, nr Tingwall
Iron Age (100 BC AD) broch still over 10 ft high surrounded by other buildings and rock cut ditch. (AM). Admission at standard times. Entry fee charged.

2 Brough of Birsay
Tidal island containing ruined Romanesque church and remains of Viking longhouse complex. Also remains of 8-9th C Celtic church and graveyard, the hall of the Mighty Earl Thorfinn (11th C) and the cathedral he built there. Admission at standard hours. Entry fee charged. (AM).

3 Click Mill, Dounby
Only surviving example of horizontal water mill of Norse origin. Still in working condition. Admission at all times. No entry fee (AM).

4 Dwarfie Stone, Hoy
A rock-cut sandstone tomb unique in Britain, dating from about 2000-1600 BC. Admission at all times. No entry fee charged. (AM).

5 Maeshowe Chambered Cairn
Dates from 2000 BC. The most magnificent chambered tomb in Western Europe and contains the largest collection of runic inscriptions to be found in any one place in the world left by Viking raiders. Admission standard hours. Entry fee charged.

6 Midhowe Broch, Rousay
Iron Age (100 BC-200 AD) broch and walled enclosure containing other buildings. Admission at all times. No entry fee charged. (AM).

6 Midhowe Stalled Cairn, Rousay
Megalithic (2000-1800 BC) chambered tomb divided into twelve compartments containing stone slab benches. Described as an "elongated ship of death". (AM). Admission at all times. No entry fee charged.

7 Skara Brae Prehistoric Village
Dwellings dating from 2500-2000 BC preserved with stone furniture, hearths and drains by drift sand. Admission at standard times. Entry fee charged. Complex stone age village of ten one-roomed houses.

8 Standing Stones of Stenness and Ring of Brodgar
Two circles of upright stones with enclosing ditches dating from about 1800 BC. Bronze Age. Admission at all times. No entry fee charged.

9 Unstan Chambered Cairn
Neolithic burial chamber (1800 BC) in which fragments of pottery bowls were found. Suggests a fusion of both chambered and stalled cairn construction and thus perhaps two different cultures. (AM). No entry fee charged.

Shetland

1 Clickhimin Broch, Lerwick
Site first occupied in late Bronze Age, fortified in Iron Age and broch built at later date. (AM).

2 Jarlshof, Sumburgh
Remains of three extensive village settlements, dating from Bronze Age, Iron Age and Viking period. (AM). Entry fee charged.

3 Mousa Broch
Best preserved example of the Iron Age brochs peculiar to Scotland, still standing over 40 ft high. Visit by boat from Sandwick. (AM).

4 Ness of Burgi
Defensive stone structure of Iron Age. (AM).

5 St Ninian's Isle
Site of 5th C church where priceless silver plate was found in 1958.

6 Staneydale, Walls
Neolithic or Bronze Age 'heel' shaped structure containing large oval chamber. (AM).

⭐ GEOGRAPHICAL FEATURES

Orkney

1 Old Man of Hoy
Detached tower of Old Red Sandstone 450 ft high.

2 Red Head, Eday
Sea bird colony. (See also BIRD SANCTUARIES AND OBSERVATION POINTS).

3 St John's Head, Hoy
Vertical sea cliff, 1136 ft high. The highest perpendicular cliff face in UK.

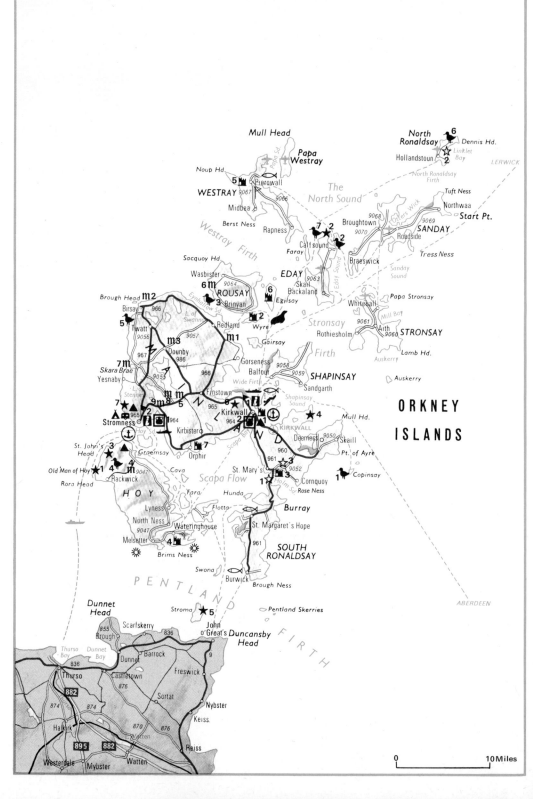

4 The Gloup
Cliff cave which can be visited by boat. Geological structure on high cliffs — a large opening under which visits can be made by boat.

5 Stroma
Although shown on this map Stroma is in fact Caithness' only island.

6 Wideford Hill, St Ola
Viewpoint, 3 miles from Kirkwall, giving views of nearly whole island group.

7 Yesnaby Castle, Sandwick
A detached tower of Old Red Sandstone standing on two legs.

Shetland

1 Foula Cliffs
Quarter mile high cliff with 'The Kame' seabird breeding colony.

2 Mavis Grind
The neck of land where the North Sea and the Atlantic come within a stone's throw of each other.

3 Muckle Flugga
Most northerly island of British Isles. View from Saxavourd Hill.

4 Ramna Stacks
Pinnacles of rock at North Roe.

5 'The Drongs', 'The Grind of Navir' and 'Holes of Scraada'
Spectacular cliff features in the Esha Ness peninsula.

📷 MUSEUMS

Orkney

1 Stromness Museum
Natural history and New Stone Age exhibits. Normally during the summer months special exhibitions are mounted on facets of Orcadian life, eg ships and steam, crafts, lighthouses, etc. Open: July-Aug (open 10 am); other times, Mon-Sat, 11 am to 12.30 pm; 1.30 pm to 5 pm; Thurs, 11 am to 1 pm only. No entry fee charged.

2 Tankerness House Museum, Kirkwall
House built in 1574. Depicts life in Orkney throughout 4000 years. Open Mon-Sat, 10.30 am to 1 pm; 2 pm to 5 pm. No entry fee charged.

Shetland

1 Croft Museum, South Voe, Dunrossness
Original croft house, out-buildings and water mill, depicting life in Shetland in the mid 19th century. Entry fee charged.

2 Shetland County Museum, Lerwick
Comprehensive range of exhibits covering the islands' history from the Iron Age onwards. No entry fee charged.

☆ OTHER PLACES OF INTEREST

Orkney

1 Churchill Barriers
Four causeways built in Second World War to seal up eastern approaches to Scapa Flow naval base. Now used as roadways linking the islands.

2 Island dyke and sheep, North Ronaldsay
Due to limited area of land on island, a huge 6 ft dyke was built around North Ronaldsay, outside of which the sheep are kept. The sheep eat the seaweed and its high iodine content has now been built into the breed genetically. They need iodine to live

3 Norwood Collection of Antiques, Holm
Private collection of antiques. Open 2 pm to 7 pm. Entry fee charged.

🐦 BIRD SANCTUARIES AND OBSERVATION POINTS

Orkney

1 Copinsay
Sea bird reserve dedicated to naturalist and broadcaster James Fisher. Owned by World Wildlife Fund, managed by RSPB in addition to their own three reserves at Dale of Cottascarth, Birsay Moors and Hobbister.

2 Eday and Calf of Eday
Fulmars and cormorants.

3 Eynhallow
Fulmars.

4 Hoy
Birds of cliff and moorland.

5 Marwick Head, Birsay
Sea birds. One of the most important sea bird colonies with different species confining themselves to different ledges at various levels.

6 North Ronaldsay
Migration watch point.

7 Red Head of Eday and Grey Head
Both sea bird colonies.

Shetland

1 Fair Isle
Bird observatory, key migration point, seabird colonies. (FIBOT, NTS) (See also NATIONAL TRUST FOR SCOTLAND ESTATES).

2 Fetlar
Snowy owls, breeding waders, sea-birds and skuas. (RSPB).

3 Foula
Skuas, gannets, Manx shearwaters, puffins.

4 Hermaness
Skuas, gannets, guillemots and puffins. (NCC). (See also NATIONAL NATURE RESERVES).

5 Noss
Super sea-bird colony, especially gannets. (NCC/RSPB). (See also NATIONAL NATURE RESERVES).

6 Sumburgh Head
Sea-birds on cliffs and migrants — eg Pool of Virkie.

ℹ TOURIST INFORMATION CENTRES

Orkney

1 Kirkwall
Information Centre, Castle Street. Tel: 0856 2856 Telex: 75171.

2 Stromness (S)
Ferry Terminal Building, Stromness. Tel: 0856 85716

Shetland

1 Lerwick
Alexandra Wharf. Tel: Lerwick 0595 3434.

NATIONAL NATURE RESERVES

Shetland

1 Haaf Gruney
A low, green, fertile islet with a flora resembling that of similar areas of Serpentine rock on Unst. Storm petrels breed here. Common and grey seals plentiful. (NCC).

2 Hermaness
Reserve includes Muckle Flugga. Of great ornithological importance and noted for the breeding of the great skuas. Puffins. (NCC). (See also BIRD SANCTUARIES AND OBSERVATION POINTS).

3 Noss
Island with great cliffs that are the breeding ground of hosts of sea-birds. Visit from Lerwick (NCC/RSPB). (See also BIRD SANCTUARIES AND OBSERVATION POINTS).

NATIONAL TRUST FOR SCOTLAND ESTATES

Shetland

Fair Isle
Most isolated inhabited island in Britain. Important bird breeding colony with observatory. Visit twice weekly by boat from Grutness (Shetland) or charter aircraft from Sumburgh (FIBOT and NTS). (See also BIRD SANCTUARIES AND OBSERVATION POINTS).

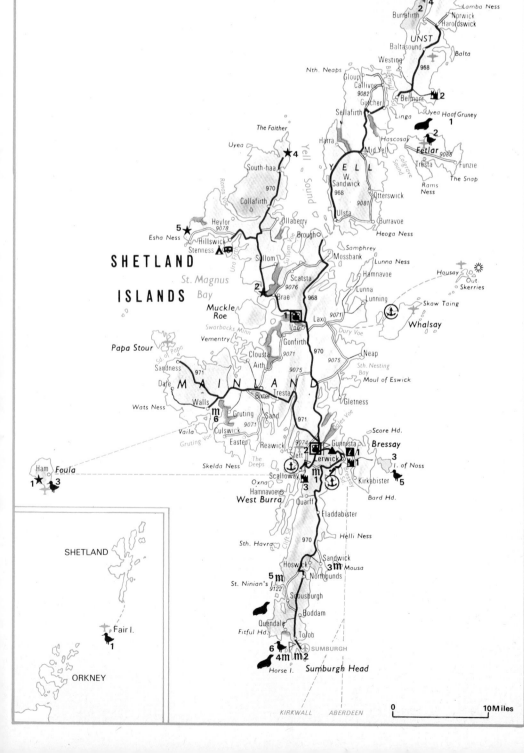

SHETLAND ISLANDS

MAINLAND

0   10 Miles
KIRKWALL   ABERDEEN

SHETLAND

ORKNEY